The Jesus of Jericho

The Jesus of Jericho:

The Good Samaritan in the Public Square

By George Harold Trudeau

Stonewall Publishing, LLC

Copyright © 2022 by Stonewall Publishing, LLC

All rights reserved. No part of this book may be reproduced or used in any manner without written permission of the copyright owner except for use of quotations in a book review.

ISBN: 978-1-7366130-4-7

Unless otherwise noted, Scripture quotations come from the English Standard Version®, ESV®, Copyright 2016 © by Crossway.®

Other Scripture quotations come from the New International Version®, NIV®, Copyright 2011 © by Biblica, Inc.®

Book cover design by Drew Wilson.

*To my wife who supported me
to the parents who raised me
to the teachers who mastered the craft of the word
and encouraged me along the way.*

*To the Blessed Trinity who saved me
and to the One, Holy, Catholic, and Apostolic Faith
which nourished me.*

Contents

Introduction   8

Part I: The Kingdom

1. Orthodoxy and Insanity   23
2. Contracts and Covenants   34
3. Truth and Tribalism   45
4. Ethical Pragmatism   58
5. Regulating Pragmatism   65
6. Pursuing the Dream   76

Part II: The King

7. Jesus and the Abstract Theologian   89
8. The Broken Road   96
9. The New Jerusalem   120

Bibliography   132

Introduction

The Position of a Christian in an Insane World

> This thing which I have called for convenience the *Tao*, and which others may call Natural Law or Traditional Morality or the First Principles of Practical Reason or the First Platitudes, is not one among a series of possible systems of value. It is the sole source of all value judgments. If it is rejected, all value is rejected. If any value is retained, it is retained.
>
>   C.S. Lewis, *The Abolition of Man*

> Your kingdom come,
> Your will be done,
> on earth as it is in heaven.
>
>   Jesus of Nazareth, *Sermon on the Mount*

A Christian is a citizen of two worlds and therefore has a duplex, and at times dichotomous, commitment to his nation and the kingdom of God. In relation to the nation, the Political Christian seeks to implement general, preventative, moralities through indirect relationship and reason. In relation to the kingdom of God, the Christian seeks to Christianize the culture through direct relationship, bottom-up, spiritual regeneration, resulting in life change. The two commitments are distinct but not necessarily dichotomous; hence, they are a duplex commitment.

A duplex has two active residencies in one house. Much like a duplex, the life of a Christian is dual residency. Stanley Hauerwas and William H. Willimon described the position of a Christian as a *Resident Alien* in their book title of the same name. Christians are both totally residing in their locality, and foreign to their home in a paradoxical way. In this book, I use the term Political Christian to suggest every Christian is socio-politically situated. The Political Christian is an embodied soul formed, for better or worse, by a social location. No Christian is apolitical. In James K. A. Smith's book series *Cultural Liturgies,* he says the public is not a spatial location, but an era and way of being, which actively forms and deforms us through its own *liturgical* practices. The material practices of the public form our affections. According to Smith, the church is a political reality that reforms our social imaginary through liturgy (habitual practices). The church is ushering in the only ultimately real beloved community in an era of transient earthly kingdoms. While Smith's series describe posture rather than policy, he sees Christian aspects to Liberalism (liberal democracies) that can be promoted in the various public squares throughout the earth.[1]

At the same time, the Political Christian's identity is in Christ and their permanent citizenship is in heaven. The liturgical practices of heaven— hearing God's Word, the Sacraments, offering prayers, and giving to the poor— reform and sanctify God's people. While it is true that from belief flows action, practice also forms belief. As the ancient Christian axiom states, *Lex Orandi, Lex Credendi,* or "the law of what is prayed is the law of what is believed." How we worship impacts how we understand God, and our practices shape the journey on the road to Jericho.

---

[1] See James K. A. Smith, *Awaiting the King: Reforming Public Theology,* (Grand Rapids: Baker Academic, 2017).

In the story of the Good Samaritan, Jesus discloses to His covenant people how they are to be salt and light in a world of darkness. The Christian must wrestle with this dialectical dance of heaven and earth until we await the final state of the kingdom of God. The Samaritan worked to restore a broken man to wholeness. His identity was not informed by the broken world, but he understood he had a responsibility to better his social location.

Part I: The Kingdom provides a roadmap for citizens in Christ's kingdom as people who must walk the Bloody Way of Jericho without losing their heavenly identity. The scope of this book sets out to apply political or public theology to the issues of racial reconciliation. Reconciliation is not only a concern in the United States but an ancient concern in the Jew-Gentile divide of the early church, and a contemporary, global phenomenon. Desmond Tutu sought South African reconciliation in a culture ravaged by Apartheid. Father Ubald's legacy sets out to reconcile the Tutsis and Hutus after the Rwandan genocide. While we mourn over the continued strife of Cain and Abel, we take heart because we are not struggling alone; we are struggling with our brothers and sisters throughout the world. Jesus gives a model of neighbor love and reconciliation in the parable of the Good Samaritan that is both moral and practical, subverting the sentimentality and abstraction theology approaches of His day.

Part II: The King overviews the character and practice of Christ as He works to reconcile all things to Himself on the Bloody Way to Jericho. Reconciliation is at the heart of the gospel with both a vertical and horizontal component. Reconciliation between people is not one-sided assimilation of a minority culture into a majority culture. Godly reconciliation is an integration of equals. J. Deotis Roberts's book, *Liberation and Reconciliation,* argues that liberation from the inferior-superior mindset must logically precede racial reconciliation between races. Robert's book was from a generation concerned with the Black Power movement, similar to the currents of the Black Lives Matter movement today. Reconciliation is the nature of Christ's ministry, which reconciles lost people through the cross. Reconciliation is not an ultimate goal, but a penultimate means to bring about a Christian family. God is a reconciler because God is love and love is the final Christian vision. In the end, God's covenantal promise will be fulfilled in familial unity:

> *"I will give them a heart to know that I am the LORD,*
> *and they shall be my people and I will be their God."*
> —Jeremiah 24:7

I chose the issues of segregation as a snapshot of how the duplex vision could be applied. In many ways, the civil rights movement is the new plumb line of religion and politics where people position themselves. The civil rights movement captures the problem of churches absolving their duty in their public square. Churches are haunted by their complicity in oppressive structures during slavery and Jim Crow; or not haunted at all. Young people are grappling with the sins of their fathers in a globalizing world. The disenfranchised want a solid faith that is also publicly prophetic. Given the political detachment of many mainstream Protestants and Catholics, many are looking to subversive public theologians like Desmond Tutu, Martin Luther King Jr., James Cone, Oscar Romero, Gustavo Gutiérrez, and Mohandas Gandhi to explain their political and spiritual situation. Unfortunately, many of these leaders adopt biblical anthropology, and provide valid social analysis, but they fail to hold up the equally important biblical Christology and Christocentrism— that it is Christ the God-man who is reconciling all things to Himself. Christ is both the means and the end of all life.

People are looking for a political faith, but they commit spiritual suicide the moment faith is placed in politics. It is evident we must abhor the religion of the slave master that told their slaves to look beyond for hope, leaving them barren for the here and now. Therefore, the purpose of public and political theology is for the church to stand on the promises of God as they live out His agenda of love and justice in the public square. It is not to say that people go too far in politics, but if one relies on mere political mechanisms, they will hit a wall in the march of inevitable progress because of competing interests.

As Beneatha says in Lorraine Hansberry's *A Raisin in the Sun,* "Don't you see there isn't any real progress…there is only one large circle that we march in, around and around, each of us with our own little picture in front of us—our own little mirage that we think is the future."[2] Progressive visions of history assume the

---

[2] Lorraine Hansberry, *A Raisin in the Sun,* (New York:

perspective of an objective moral standard above finite visions. Moreover, human effort without the power of God cannot consummate cosmic justice because humanism cannot bring qualitative changes in human nature, only quantitative changes. Progressivism baselessly posits changes as positive developments in human nature. Additionally, without an objective moral standard to work towards, there is no way of knowing whether or not one is progressing or regressing. Lastly, Progressivism appropriates a Christian vision of history without the condition of faith in Christ. Christian history is conditionally progressive. By accepting Christ's offer of salvation, people can experience qualitative, spiritual changes. In the end, Christ's kingdom will be fully realized and there will be peace on earth. Yet, the Christian utopia is not inevitable; it is conditional, based on Christ.

Political theology is a mere specification in a larger system of theology rooted in God's salvation history. In reality, public theology is more of an admission than a stand-alone field of study. When God saves, He declares the child of God as just; but then begins the work of sanctification, where God makes the child of God just in

---

Vintage Books, 1994) 134.

practice. Christians become burdened for the lost, the widow, and the orphan. A follower goes beyond solidarity and monetary funds, into personal involvement in the lives of God's creatures. Political theology admits that God's commands move out beyond personal devotion into public life.

In the story of the Good Samaritan, the Samaritan involves himself totally and sacrificially in the life of a beaten and forsaken man amidst a sea of indifference. The model Christ gives of ethical living is one of direct action and personal involvement, but Christ also advocates for indirect, social action as well. While Christians must strive to be non-partisan, they should never be impartial and uninvolved. Followers of Christ move past mental assent because God is not an apolitical, nonactive, inoffensive therapist with a sterile message of good feelings. God is an active liberator, redeemer, and savior Who entered history to involve Himself in the lives of His people. Discipleship begins with liberation: Jesus said, "if the Son sets you free, you will be free indeed" (John 8:36). Freedom is the midwife to transformation.

Transformation occurs in individuals, in collective groups, and in the social fabric of cultures. In the book of

Acts, a revival broke out among Jews and Greeks resulting in conversion (Acts 17:3-4). They were individually saved, as well as collectively saved in response to Paul's preaching. In response, there were Jews who did not convert and decided to form a mob to attack the house of Jason in search of Paul and Silas (Acts 17:5). Instead, the mob captured Jason and other Christians because they supported Paul. The mob condemned the works of Paul and Silas saying, "These men who have turned the world upside down" (Acts 17:6). Just as Jesus threatened the religious establishment, so did Paul and the early church. The mass conversions weakened the religious establishment's influence and power over people. Jesus was also a threat to Caesar because the gospel teaches that Jesus is greater than he and that Caesar must submit to King Jesus. God's works are never isolated. His supernatural acts of recreation ripple across creation. When God rescued Israel from the clutches of Egypt, He antagonized the political agenda of Pharaoh, disrupted the economic system of the Egyptians, and warred with a kingdom of brother exploitation. Christian liberty distinguishes from libertarians, Jacobins, and America First ideologues. God declares a teleological end to liberation, "Let my people go, that they may serve me in the wilderness" (Ex. 7:16). Freedom is a gift of God, for the glory of God. Freedom is the ability to live out God's commands. Without Christ, there is no freedom for we are enslaved to our sins and passions.

Jesus gave a dream in the form of prayer: "on earth as it is in heaven." God is at work in history making earth like heaven. All theology begins with God's manifestation in history, especially in the Incarnation of Christ. In the final state, Jesus's people will worship in unity, and diversity, as one people: "After this I looked, and there before me was a great multitude that no one could count, from every nation, tribe, people and language, standing before the throne and before the Lamb" (Rev. 7:9 NIV). Followers of Christ must follow in the footsteps of Jesus in the public arena declaring Jesus's vision of humanity. But this dream can only be achieved through the Lamb of God who takes away the sin of the world (John 1:29). Sin is separation from God, from life, and from other people. Jesus is the Good Physician who destroys the corrosive cancer of sin without destroying the sinner. Through the Lamb of God, we have the beloved community.

Jesus's dream captured the imagination of Martin Luther King Jr. within his black Baptist tradition. On the steps of the Lincoln Memorial, in the one-hundred-year shadow of the Emancipation Proclamation, King declared his dream of the beloved community, "I have a dream that one day on the red hills of Georgia, the sons of former slaves and the sons of former slave owners will be able to sit down together at the table of brotherhood." While King's call for brotherhood may sound like a mere call for national reform through human means, the speech takes an eschatological and supernatural turn: "I have a dream that one day every valley shall be exalted, every hill and mountain shall be made low, the rough places will be made plain, and the crooked places will be made straight, and the glory of the Lord shall be revealed, and all flesh shall see it together."[3] The final vision is for the justice of God to be realized in every facet of life. God must make every crooked place straight in the end. Only in the second coming of Christ will this dream be realized. This dream does not produce complacency, as is evident in the

---

[3] Martin Luther King Jr., "I Have a Dream," *National Archives,* Aug. 28, 1963. https://www.archives.gov/files/social-media/transcripts/transcript-march-pt3-of-3-2602934.pdf

active ministry of King and other civil rights Christians. The dream is the victory cry that motivates the Christian until the end.

We must prayerfully consider how God will use us in the public square, but not fear, not cower, and not retreat from the uncertainties of this world. We must not confuse consideration with complacency. For certain, there can be a time for a Christian to retreat into the wilderness of prayer and reflection; but only for a moment. Eventually, the Christian must come out of the wilderness and travel on the Bloody Way to Jericho. We will meet people to help, people to rob us, or be the person in need of healing. On the dangerous road to Jericho, Christ will be there aiding the Political Christian in making this earthly dwelling a reflection of His heavenly kingdom.

Part I
The Kingdom

Chapter 1

Orthodoxy & Insanity

> A cosmic philosophy is not constructed to fit a man; a cosmic philosophy is constructed to fit a cosmos.
> G.K. Chesterton, Introduction to the Book of Job

> Perhaps (in short) this extraordinary thing is really the ordinary thing; at least the normal thing, the center. Perhaps, after all, it is Christianity that is sane and all its critics that are mad — in various ways.
> G.K. Chesterton, *Orthodoxy*

Extremes breed extremes in political climates of fear. Polarization fuels its own fire and spreads to the hearts of even the most careful and cautious. The flames of social media have spread the lie that adopting wholesale ideologies is the only way to be effectively involved in politics. Social media and political campaigns have convinced users that there are two sides instead of 330,000,000 citizens. How is it possible that bipartisan politics, led by the few, can so easily hypnotize the masses into believing that the way they define conversations is the only acceptable way to define social life? Time has passed for anyone to be convinced of the gnostic heresy in the realm of politics. The attitude of white churches during the civil rights movement to merely concern itself with spiritual matters, not political matters, was really a gnostic, individualized, spirituality that allowed white supremacist politics to define race relations. In short, by adopting a *status quo* Conservatism, the church really accepted theological Liberalism. American churches should have been the first social institutions to integrate because God's church is one and the dividing wall of hostility has been broken down by the crucified and resurrected Christ.

Fortunately, what lacked in the white church was made up for in the black church. Many conservative, black churches knew the gospel had a social imperative and black churches became the epicenters of desegregation. Dexter Avenue Baptist Church in Montgomery, Alabama was founded by Pastor-Theologian Charles Octavius Boothe (1845-1924).[4] Boothe was what many would a

Fundamentalist for his unashamed belief in the historic doctrines of Christianity, and for preaching the Bible as God's Word. Boothe was a former slave who taught other formerly enslaved African Americans how to read so they could know the whole counsel of God's Word and free them from racial myths previously taught. Slave masters often prevented the enslaved from being clergy and would usually read texts out of Paul's epistles, specifically the passages that dealt with slavery. Boothe's literacy ministry was a form of social uplift, believing that education was essential for the advancement of African Americans, as well as for the sanctification of a Christian. Boothe would also help establish Selma College for the purpose of training ministers and freemen. In sum, Boothe and other African American ministers were of the persuasion that their calling was to preach the gospel, while also promoting social uplift for their congregants.

In 1954, Martin Luther King Jr. became the newly installed pastor at Dexter and he immediately sought to reform the classist attitude of Dexter to be more inclusive.

---

[4] See Charles Octavius Boothe, *Plain Theology for Plain People,* Introduction by Walter R. Strickland II, (Bellingham: Lexham Press, 2017).

He established social programs at the church which would serve as outreach programs to the community. King Jr. learned from his father King Sr. (Daddy King) who was a fundamentalist social gospeler. Daddy King led a voting rights campaign in Atlanta, Georgia thirty years before his son would involve himself in the Civil Rights Act of 1965. Under King Jr.'s leadership, Dexter became the epicenter of the Montgomery Bus Boycott, which sparked the civil rights movement.

King's Social Gospel was a form of Christian Nationalism intent on saving the soul of America from the threefold tyranny of racial discrimination, poverty, and war. King Jr. strayed from a historic Christian upbringing by implementing Liberal Protestantism in his faith. Similarly, the Moral Majority in the 1970s formed to fight social evils like the loss of religious liberty and the legalization of abortion. Often, right-wing Christian Nationalism sees itself as the preserver of Judeo-Christian values in the United States, which was founded on those principles.

When the church is uninvolved, or delays correcting corrosive issues like segregation, it becomes easy for other humanistic ideologies to take the reins and become the spiritual leaders of dissatisfied people. Suspending the social imperative also leads to leaders going too far in correcting the issue as is the case for King who was dissatisfied with the lack of leadership of the church in the public square. Even so, the issue is not dissatisfaction. The issue is that people fail to take their dissatisfaction to its logical conclusion: the myths that human ideologies tell are too small for God's big world.

G.K. Chesterton speaking of the insanity of every worldview says, "A small circle is quite as infinite as a large circle; but, though it is quite as infinite, it is not so large. In the same way the insane explanation is quite as complete as the sane one, but it is not so large. A bullet is quite as round as the world, but it is not the world."[5] Only God's Word is sufficient enough to explain humanity without reducing humanity. At its core, all extremism stems from narrative simplicity. Humanity creates systems of thought that use one line of reasoning applied to every situation, thus reducing humanity and oversimplifying issues. In Marxist thought, all of life is a product of

---

[5] G.K. Chesterton, "Orthodoxy," In *The Three Apologies of G.K. Chesterton: Heretics, Orthodoxy & The Everlasting Man*, 249–451, (Bristol: Mockingbird Press, 2018), 139.

economic class discrimination. In Freudian thought, all of life's issues revolve around subconscious suppression. In Christian Fundamentalism, only the spiritual world matters. The only way to dismantle extremes is to inject a healthy dose of dissatisfaction and doubt into their mythos, and thus disrupt the narrative simplicity. Only through bearing the cross of disillusionment can we walk in the newness of Christian imagination— having a worldview that soars the heights and plumb the depths of God's world.

Many well-intended Christians witness the impurity of Christian Nationalism and how it pollutes the message of Christ. In response, many adopt a withdrawal approach and preach an apolitical gospel. It is very unclear how Christians should involve themselves in public conversations since Christians are either too partisan to be Christian or too idealistic to be useful. What follows is a solution by providing useful principles for a Christian that avoid the following pitfalls and reveal that every theology has a political component. Some of the political approaches to the Political Christian are: The Cynical Approach, The Conformity Approach, The Cloudy Approach.

The Cynical Approach says, *Since there is no way to fix all the social problems there is no point for the Christian to be involved in politics.* This approach believes that the problems of social ethics are unsolvable. Many Fundamentalists detached themselves from the public square in the name of eschatology. Since the world is getting worse, the church needs to be a bomb shelter from the world. In this model, the church is a defensive subculture meant to protect one from the evils of the world. If the world is going to the dumps, there is no point in fixing it. Part of the cynical relationship many Fundamentalists had with the public square is because politics is performed through indirect relationships so it is difficult to see positive social changes. Everyone finds themselves within communities they inherited, and everyone exists interdependently with other people. Whether or not someone would admit to individual limitations, structures are important and can be improved or degraded.

The Conformity Approach does not refer to the well-known heresy of syncretizing Christianity and culture. Here, I refer to a subtler heterodoxy that suggests the Bible gives direct insight into social issues. **The Conformity Approach** says, *Since Christ has come to bring* *social justice, it is the responsibility of the church to eliminate social evils/preserve social institutions using top-down systems of change.* I refer to ideologies like the Social Gospel of Martin Luther King Jr. and John Lewis, and the Christian Right articulated by people like Jerry Falwell Sr. or Franklin Graham. White Evangelicals reacted against the cynical tendencies of Fundamentalists believing that issues like religious liberties would be lost without active engagement in politics. Unfortunately, active engagement in politics meant partisan politics. On the flip side, black Fundamentalists and black social gosplers believed the most crucial social issue for the church to protest was segregation. Conservative black churches were socially active in public issues. King's Black Social Gospel contained a natural theological component, and even a supernatural eschatological component, but his public vision of the beloved community was overly political and anthropocentric. Both the Moral Majority and the King's Social Gospel are versions of Christian Nationalism that champion the social benefits of the gospel without the biblical means of spiritual transformation. The result is a human-centered religion that Jesus critiqued during His day. Using politics to impose outward, moral, conformity communicates an artificial transformation rather than a genuine transformation resulting from gospel proclamation.

The last approach does not see an inefficiency in the world but an inefficiency in the Word to speak into politics. **The Cloudy Approach** says, *Since the Bible provides no clear answer to how Christians are to interact with politics it is best to avoid it altogether.* It is very easy to see how the Cloudy Approach could relapse into the gnostic heresy of being merely concerned with "spiritual things" but the social teachings of Jesus clearly show that Jesus wants His followers to be salt and light to a world in darkness. While the Bible does not give direct answers to all specific problems, Scripture provides practical wisdom and principles to discern the will of God. So then, how can a Christian be actively involved in politics without sacrificing the complex orthodoxy for reductive partisan politics?

The Duplexity Approach: Only through embracing a duplex commitment to her contract with the state and her covenantal commitment to God can the Political Christian maintain a principled, yet, practical orthodoxy that leads to human flourishing. The Political

Christian must first and foremost be involved in the micro institutions of family, church, education, and non-profit organizations through gospel proclamation and ethical living as a first means of social ethics. Direct Christian action is the Christian's primary responsibility as covenantal members of God's church. As secondary means of social ethics, the Christian must involve themselves in their contractual obligations to the state. Since we live in a world of interdependence, the Christian should consider the best macro structures for micro institutions to operate under. The Political Christian must use reason and revelation to consider the best practical policies that are fair for all people.

Chapter 2

Contracts & Covenants

So whatever you wish that others would do to you, do also to them, for this is the Law and the Prophets.
>Matthew 7:12

Then Jesus said to them, "Give back to Caesar what is Caesar's and to God what is God's."
>Matthew 12:17

A Christian has two residencies and two allegiances in this world— their nation and the kingdom of God— and these allegiances are both true in their proper order. The commitment to the nation is contractual, conditional, and based on skepticism. The commitment to the kingdom is covenantal, unconditional, and based on love. At times these commitments are at odds, but when they are not, the Christian should find a happy unity with these duplex commitments. The Apostle Paul commands the Romans to obey their government as part of their spiritual commitment to God, "Let every person be subject to the governing authorities" (Rom. 13:1). Paul even identifies himself as a Roman citizen in Acts when he was unjustly flogged (Acts 22:25). Even more than his identification as a Roman citizen was his ethnic identity as a Jew. Paul says, "For I could wish that I myself were cursed and cut off from Christ for the sake of my people, those of my own race, the people of Israel" (Rom. 9:3-4 NIV). Paul had a special love for his kinsmen that is even more present in his writings than his Roman identity. Scripture teaches that it is morally right to have commitments toward socio-cultural structures like government and cultural heritage. However, allegiance to government and culture is temporary and conditional because of the Christian's higher allegiance and citizenship.

    The Apostle Paul's identity is further explained in his letter to the Philippians where he identifies his primary citizenship as heaven. Paul says, "But our citizenship is in heaven, and from it we await a Savior, the Lord Jesus Christ" (Phil. 3:20). The Christian is more closely identified as a son of God than he is a son of Rome or son of Israel because only God is absolute. Ethnicity, nationality, and family are not absolute commitments. Since Christ is Lord over all, He defines our role in family, state, and culture. At times the Christian's allegiances are tested and competing. In a perfect world, the Christian's relationships would never compete; they would be in shalom. In a broken world, the Christian will at times have to sacrifice one relationship for the sake of another. Not all relationships are equal in priority but the prioritizing of relationships does not negate the commitment. For example, political allegiance and allegiance to God compete in the book of Acts. Peter exclaims to the Sanhedrin, "We must obey God rather than men." (Acts 5:29). At first glance, this verse suggests the Christian should adopt the Cynical Approach because of the depravity of man as well as the absurd contradictions in a fallen world. However, it is important to remember the previous example in Acts where Paul uses his political identity for just purposes (Acts 22:25). With Paul's Roman defense, the Christian may be swayed to The Conformity Approach, where political power is used to bring about God's justice. At the very least, Acts condemns any notion of an apolitical Christian. But what is the Christian supposed to do with the apparent selective political allegiance? Does the selectivity suggest a nominal commitment? The Political Christian does not have a nominal commitment to their nation but a conditional commitment.

According to the political tradition of Liberalism defined largely by John Locke (1632-1704), citizens decide to be governed on a bilateral contract using natural law. Natural law is the common grace inherent to every human by merit of God's creative power. Everyone is fallen, but all are still made in God's image. As will be seen in the next section, Liberalism is not inherently Christian, but Liberalism can be seen as a negative morality that allows positive Christian morality to blossom. The instinct of many political Christians is to Christianize political systems. To not Christianize the government is to compromise. In this model, conformity is seen as the default mode for Christian involvement in politics. However, is this the only available avenue for Christians? By utilizing the wisdom of Locke, Christians can avoid an authoritarian approach to political involvement through the principle of consensual governance. Scripture speaks of general moralities that Christians can refer to when implementing public law.

Some examples of general moralities in Scripture are the creation ordinances (Gen. 1-2), the Noahide laws (Gen 9:4-8), the conscience (Rom. 2:15), and of course the universal golden rule (Matt. 7:12). From these general moral codes, humanity can contractually set up governments that prevent immorality, i.e. murder and theft. From here the church can come in to prescribe specific morals like tithing and sacraments. By nature, governmental morality must be involuntary for it to be enforced. By nature, Christian morality must be voluntary to be loving. By providing a framework for lost people to live in safe conditions, Christian morality can come into the culture to provide the missing piece. When considering a public theology, one has to appeal to the better angels of human nature, which, according to God's word, has a conscience and an ability to understand basic moral structures despite their sinfulness (Matt. 7:11). Legally, it is possible to call everyone to a standard of decency. But, it would be wrong to appeal to a strictly Christian conscience at a political level because God had differentiated the roles and responsibilities of the state and church. Spiritually, it is impossible to ask unbelievers to behave like Christians.

Rather than relying on a top-down system of change through governmental power as the Conformity Approach suggests, the Christian community utilizes spiritual renewal through the proclamation of the gospel. The gospel, and the gospel alone, is the power of God unto salvation (Rom. 1:16). Before the Apostles were commissioned they had to "stay in the city until you are clothed with power from on high" for only through the supernatural power of the Holy Spirit can qualitative change be brought to human nature (Lk. 24:49). The Apostle Paul says, "Therefore, if anyone is in Christ, he is a new creation. The old has passed away; behold, the new has come" (2 Cor. 5:17). It is God's purpose that those who have been transformed by God's love model His fatherly care for the widow and orphan (Ps. 68:5; Jm. 1:17). Simultaneously, Christians are to honor governing authorities and even pray for governments because Christ died for all (1 Tim. 2:1-6). The Political Christian must distinguish his relationship to the church and his nation in the same way a man distinguishes his role as a husband and father. The roles may differ in their dedication and responsibilities, but one commitment is not negated by another.

Abraham Kuyper's concept of sphere sovereignty clarifies how different situations in life call for differing ethical responses. In Christian ethics, God's moral character is the foundation of all ethics, and context is merely one aspect of applying God's Word. Kuyper states that the "Triune God as the only and absolute Sovereign" and "this exalted Sovereign delegated and does delegate His authority to human beings."[6] From God's authority stems other authorities such as the family (Eph. 3:15), state (Rom 13:1), and church (Matt. 16:19) (the list is not exhaustive). Since authority is granted by God, all authority should be seen as grace to be stewarded by God's creatures. Authoritarianism is the lie that authority is inherent to certain individuals rather than inherited from God. Therefore, Christians must abhor any form of abuse of power or entitlement to power.

Spheres are defined by their limitations and responsibilities. A father is permitted to send his child to a

---

[6] Abraham Kuyper, George Kamps, Translator, "Sphere Sovereignty," (Inaugural Address at *Free University,* October 20, 1880), 4.

corner for a time-out, but a father may not send a Judge to time-out for being too loud with a gavel. A police officer is permitted to arrest a criminal, but a police officer is confined to their jurisdiction. In God's world, situations within spheres merits differentiating ethics. In the Old Testament, God commands parents to catechize their children (Deut. 6:7), but parents are forbidden to kill their children as a punishment for sin. God commands parents with rebellious children to take their children to the elders to be stoned: "They shall say to the elders, 'This son of ours is stubborn and rebellious. He will not obey us. He is a glutton and a drunkard.' Then all the men of his town are to stone him to death" (Deut. 21:20-21 NIV). While one may think this verse is barbaric, it must be understood that there is a limitation placed on parents in this passage. Filicide was legislatively permissible in many ancient codes even going well into the Roman Empire. But God is clear, parents do not have absolute authority over their children, they must submit to their governing authorities.[7] Since parental power is limited, it is confined to a "sphere."

---

[7] For a fuller explanation of some of the difficult laws of the Torah see: Dennis Prager, edited by Joseph Telushkin, *Deuteronomy: God, Blessings, and Curses,* (Washington D.C.: Regent Faith, 2022).

Likewise, the state is confined to a sphere of responsibility. If the state tries to enforce a law that is contrary to the Word of God the law must be disobeyed. Moreover, there are laws that are quite impossible for the state to enforce for there exists an impenetrable inner life that God has given each image bearer sovereignty over: "There is a domain of thought in which no law may prevail except the law of logic. A domain of conscience where none may exercise sovereign rule except the Holy One."[8] Since there is a realm of unenforceable ethics, freedom is a human necessity. There are some matters that are only between an individual and God.

The church has been given a sphere: to make disciples of all nations. The responsibilities God has given are baptizing disciples, teaching, and going to the nations to bear witness— the state has not been given this sphere (Matt. 28:18-20). Although there are no geographical limits given to the church's sphere, Christ tells His followers, "Give back to Caesar what is Caesar's and to God what is God's" meaning Christians are not above the law so they should acknowledge whoever is in power (Matt. 12:17 NIV). Acknowledge does not mean like,

---

[8] Kuyper, "Sphere Sovereignty," 6.

endorse, or even always obey the person in power. Christians are to see that the office is bigger than the person occupying the office. Christ also limits the role of the government in the passage, for God's image is on Caesar and so are all his subjects. Therefore, Caesar must submit to God, and the subjects submit to Caesar. It is not a good testimony for a Christian to come into a foreign nation with no intent to respect or follow the laws of the nation. While going to the nations, Christians must submit to each governmental sphere and obey as much as they are able. Submission is not just morally right, but it is common sense if you are serving in a hostile environment where anything you do can be used as an opportunity to discredit Christ. Translated: Get arrested for the gospel; not for stupidity. Nor should an emigrating Christian come in with the intent to force the gospel through legal action or military might. Christians are not meant to Lord the gospel over others using political power, but to testify about Christ with the power of the gospel (Rom. 1:16).

Chapter 3

Truth & Tribalism

Liberals organized in the 60s, and conservatives certainly have a right to organize in the 80s, but it would disturb me if there was a wedding between the religious fundamentalists and the political right. The hard right has no interest in religion except to manipulate it.
  Billy Graham, *Parade Magazine*, 1981

The state of nature has a law of nature to govern it, which obliges every one: and reason, which is that law, teaches all mankind, who will but consult it, that being all equal and independent, no one ought to harm another in his life, health, liberty, or possessions.
  John Locke, *Second Treatise of Government*

Behind every party and ideology is a mythos— a way of explaining the world— and the Christian must test political myths with the Word of God. Moreover, there is not a one-to-one correlation between principles and parties. Parties are coalitions of sinful people with many worldviews. Parties are not curations of different worldviews, they are pragmatic functions of the democratic-republic. Here I will examine the big three social contract theories in Western politics which influence partisan politics today: Thomas Hobbes, John Locke, and Jean-Jacques Rousseau. All three theories tell a story about the world (a myth) which carry social imperatives.

Hobbes is the authoritarian conservative that seeks to impose law and order over depraved man. Locke is the classical liberal that seeks to provide minimal government and laws that are subjected to the natural law. Rousseau is a communitarian progressive that seeks to remove social ills that corrupt the individual. Since all these ideologies are incomplete and therefore could lead the Christian astray, it is important to test each idea within its narrative structure. Once the ideas are taken one by one, the Political Christian is free to craft a political framework that corresponds to reason and revelation.

Conservative thinkers like Edmund Burke responded to the chaotic revolution of France with reservation because it failed to keep law and order. Without a presiding governing structure that is stable and consistent, the country's citizens are headed for a tumultuous state of nature because of their wickedness. Conservatives believe that once a stable, governing structure is provided, the world can operate on some semblance of order and fairness. As a result of the strong emphasis on stability, Conservatism depicts government paternalistically most notably as the Leviathan from Thomas Hobbes's book of the same name. When governments are viewed paternalistically, the citizenry is infantilized for the sake of the elite to seize control.

As far as economics, there are differing schools of thought on the government's role, but a common value shared among most conservatives is the value of work in giving individual purpose. Generally, most conservatives will promote the idea of meritocracy and show distaste for preferential treatment, even of the lower classes. Success should be merited, not given, to allow people to contribute to their own future and society. However, meritocracy ignores that not everyone has an equal starting point and not all help creates dependency. Some preferential treatment creates autonomy and equality. For example, a disabled person will have many disadvantages, but society has set up structures that favor disabled people so they can function more easily and autonomously. Accommodations like wheelchairs, wheelchair ramps, and handicapped parking are aids to the needy. The accommodations level the playing field without creating codependency. Moreover, maintaining the *status quo* without regulating the classes, functionally promotes preferential treatment of the upper classes, and discriminatory treatment to the lower classes. All in all, Conservatism teaches people to work hard, expect good results, and pursue slow change (if any) through established structures of authority. Classical liberals will concede many of these points.

Progressivism describes the world as fundamentally innocent and equal, and it is the societal structures themselves that are unfair and oppressive. It is society and government that create inequalities and class distinctions. This account of the world puts a microscope on the outliers of society with the promise that if given the means and power, governmental action can be an equalizing force. Progressivism assumes that social change requires political force. Power must be met with power. By minimizing the role of individuals, churches, schools, and nonprofit organizations, we relegate societal responsibility to the hands of the few, creating an oligarchical rule instead of a collective society. Ironically, Progressivism is just as paternalistic as Conservatism but often avoids the criticism because Progressivism claims a purity of motives through its anti-establishment message. By paternalizing society, Progressivism dissolves the governing and citizenry into objectified beneficiaries and benefactors.

Liberalism applies to many strands of thought, including theology, but in political thought, Liberalism is a governing school that emphasizes individual rights and property. John Locke views humans as creatures capable of morality and reason, but also great evil. Government is not inherently oppressive, but it is created for clarity on property rights. Locke has a high view of creation order and under-realized fall, whereas Hobbes has a low view of creation order, and over-realized fall. Society can experience positive changes, but it can equally descend into anarchy without structure. Liberalism envisions a non-tyrannical rule through a consensual, minimal government that respects individual rights. Similar to Conservatism, once the structure is provided, Locke would say that citizens are capable of running their lives in a way that leads to flourishing.

By providing a groundwork that protects people's life, liberty, and property, people are free from the tyranny of their neighbor and the government. On a liberal model, not only are the people governed, but the governed are to be governed. The government itself is a creation of the citizenry. The people create a social contract of rules and agree to be governed by this contract, therefore the government is made for the people; not people for the government. In the United States, the Constitution is supreme law of the land, meaning that no one is above the law. The Constitution is the rule of law that defines the roles and limitations of the government. The Constitution was amended in its early stages to account for more limitations on the government. These amendments were the Bill of Rights and they laid out individual liberties that the government had to respect.

While Locke's ideology accounts for both creation and sin, morality and reason, structure and purpose, the fatal flaw of Liberalism is an overemphasis on individualism and the "free from" principle. By creating a government around "my rights," it is easy to see how someone could define freedom as selfishness rather than neighbor love. Liberalism is a compelling myth to Christians because Locke believes that law must subject itself to God's created order of individual rights. Liberalism is a system that views human individuals as moral ends, rather than societal means. However, Liberalism fails to provide a sufficient ethic for living. In the heavily individualized culture of North America, it is important to remind citizens that freedom from limitations leads to freedom to serve others. Even if the political system lends itself to an every-man-for-himself mindset, it is the duty of the Christian to model neighbor love. Rather than seeing Liberalism as the answer to the problem of narrative simplicity let us see Liberalism as partial wisdom of how to navigate the social contract non-tyrannically.

Before continuing, it is important to distinguish theological Liberalism and political Liberalism. Theological Conservatism is founded on Biblical revelation. Not only is Scripture an authority for the church, Scripture is the inerrant and infallible authority to the church. Scripture is not a textbook; it is the mind of God given to the minds of men. Christians ought to *conserve* the teachings of Scripture and apply them to everyday life. Theological Liberalism, on the other hand, strays from the teachings of Scripture, and therefore from Jesus Christ. Theological Liberalism teaches 1) a generic fatherhood of God, 2) generic brotherhood of man, 3) low Christology, and 4) low bibliology. While not all of this sounds bad, it is important to keep in mind what counterfeit currency is. Counterfeit currency can have a range of qualities and strongly resemble the real thing, but ultimately all counterfeit currency is unacceptable. To take the God-man Jesus and make Him a mere good man is not only demeaning—it is a crime against the Creator. A Christian should abhor theological Liberalism, for it shifts the authority of God and places it in the hands of the academy, religious institutions or the self. A good resource on theological Liberalism is J. Gresham Machen's Christian classic *Christianity and Liberalism*.

In these respects, we have to draw a line between political and theological Conservatism or otherwise alienate the global church. God's people across the world and across time have held a plethora of political agendas.

Politics is ever-changing; the gospel is the same every day. Many Christians were devout believers in monarchy as God's way of governing. From a traditional American-Christian perspective, monarchies are tyrannies, and tyrannical governments are liberal. Labeling tyrannies as liberal is ironic for three reasons: 1) Liberal as a colloquial adjective usually means non-traditional and has very little to do with the ideology Liberalism. 2) Monarchies are compatible within a Conservative framework given they are traditional forms of government that can provide stability. 3) Lastly, God used monarchies in His salvation history and will ultimately usher in His own monarchy. What are we to make of these conundrums? Politics is often defined by situation. Even current Conservatism exists within a liberal framework. Understanding one's own situation and the situation of others leads not only to a better understanding of ideas but a more compassionate demeanor as well.

Finally, the reason why theological and political Conservatism should not be conflated is because of the dangerous ideology of Christian Nationalism. Christian Nationalism holds the view that America is a Christian nation in an analogous way to God's covenant with Israel.

By equating American culture and politics with the gospel, we are adding a circumcision to the gospel and ultimately preaching a false gospel. God does not hold a national covenant with the United States—He holds a covenant with His universal church. The United States does not belong to Christians only. The church does not only belong to conservative Americans. God's people are ethnically and ideologically diverse. Consider Jesus's disciples: Both Simon the Zealot and Matthew the Tax Collector followed Jesus together. Simon was an anti-establishment, Zionist, who greatly opposed Rome. Matthew was an establishment, Roman civil servant. Both Simon and Matthew followed Jesus. In other words, followers of Jesus are not measured by their ballots, they are measured by faith.

Conversely, there are two brands of Christian Nationalism— one called the Christian Left, the other the Christian Right. Historically, the Christian Left gained traction in the 1960s and 1970s by people like Martin Luther King Jr. and Jimmy Carter. A more contemporary example of the Christian Left was the civil rights leader and politician John Lewis (1940-2020). Lewis was informed by the Social Gospel which saw the church as a co-conduit with the state to bring about God's kingdom on earth. While it is important for eschatology to inform ethics, the Social Gospel emphasizes political power over gospel power. Often Bible passages referring to God's covenant people like Israel or the church are applied to the United States to live and act out on a nationalistic level. The Christian Right also embraces a type of social gospel often under the guise of the preservation of freedom. The Christian Right was formed in the 1970s and 1980s by people like Jerry Falwell Sr. and Pat Robertson. The Christian Right and Christian Left use highly partisan politics to achieve their ends and so often measure faith by ballots.

Anyone who knows their need for Christ can be a Christian. Christian Nationalism acts under the guise of Conservatism, and sometimes Progressivism, but really adopts theological Liberalism. Like the Judaizers, Christian Nationalism requires a narrow political and cultural allegiance alongside faith in Christ, taking the gift of culture and heritage and making it absolute. If Paul made his Jewish heritage absolute, it is a wonder if he ever would have become a missionary to the Gentile world. The cultural addition is detrimental to the American church but also to the global Christian family, as many churches have preached a "gospel + America" leaving lasting damages on many brothers and sisters. Given the ever-changing waters of politics, and the never-changing gospel of Christ, it is paramount for Christians to radically deescalate politics from the realm of cosmic importance to that of terminable importance.

Chapter 4

Ethical Pragmatism

> Religion that is pure and undefiled before God the Father is this: to visit orphans and widows in their affliction, and to keep oneself unstained from the world.
>
> James 1:27

> There is not a square inch in the whole domain of our human life of which Christ, Who is Sovereign of all, does not cry: "Mine!"
>
> Abraham Kuyper

The Political Christian must seek to implement state policies based on natural law while also fulfilling his Christian duties based on special revelation. The Political Christian seeks to fulfill his covenantal commitment which is unconditional in its obedience. The Christian's duty to God is undivided and eternal, whereas his commitment to the state is conditioned by how much it conforms to God's law. The Political Christian is free to break a contract with the state if the state breaks the natural law or prevents God's covenantal people from fulfilling their duties. The Political Christian understands his contract with the state is only for this life, for a short period of time, but his citizenship in heaven is eternal. The Political Christian must use top-down structures to minimize injustice and that allows the covenantal people to preach and live out the gospel. The Christianization of culture is to occur through bottom-up gospel proclamation. Christianization must be voluntary so as not to encourage false conversion by force.

    The Political Christian must realize his role as a top-down system changer is one of pragmatism, not practicality. Practically, the path of the Christian is very clear— provide for the needs of the vulnerable through direct relationships. Politically, the path of the Christian is not as clear because political relationships are indirect. A Christian may be convinced that public services will do more to help the vulnerable. A Christian may be convinced that privatization and charity is the best way to help the vulnerable. At this point, the Political Christian must realize that his political opponent often wants the same goal of caring for the vulnerable but they differ on solutions. Differentiating solutions is the function of reason in the Christian's life. God gave reason to the Christian to think through what will be most beneficial for people. The Political Christian's covenant relationship is immovable because his morals are in response to voluntary relationships and direct revelation. The Political Christian's contractual commitment is moveable because his morals are in response to reason and political systems are ever-changing.

Since the Political Christian must involve herself in the policies of a fallen world, and since she herself is fallen, she should never deal with absolute idealism. Therefore, the goal of policy is improvement, not totality. Maintaining the *status quo*, for the sake of ideological purity, is complacency, not a conviction. The Political Christian is free to utilize strategies and advocate laws to change outcomes. Many African American Christians were politically involved in the civil rights movement despite Scripture's silence on the issue of American, political segregation. There was still enough Scriptural insight on the issues of racial discrimination for Christians to protest segregation laws.

In the Montgomery bus boycott, African American churches endured a yearlong boycott, kicked off by the defiance of former NAACP employee, Rosa Parks. In the struggle to desegregate public transportation, many African Americans decided to withhold money from the Montgomery bus system by carpooling, walking, and even biking as alternatives. The boycott was not desegregation, nor integration, it was a political mechanism toward desegregation. After a year of boycotting, the federal court declared that segregation was unconstitutional based on the 14th Amendment in 1956. Yet, more protections like the Civil Rights Acts of 1964 and 1965 were required to achieve more substantial equality. Arguably, there are still needs for criminal justice, education, and housing reforms to actualize the desired equality demanded by the civil rights movement. Such use of pragmatic ethics deconstructs the cartoon depiction that black religion is mere emotionalism.

In fact, the African American Christian tradition contains a streak of ethical pragmatism in both its evangelical theology and public ethics. Gayraud S. Wilmore calls Afrocentric Christianity *Pragmatic Spirituality* in his book of the same name. Wilmore states, that pragmatic spirituality, "is not particularly interested in mystical experiences, speculative theologizing, or idealizations."[9] Abstract theologians are everywhere, they existed in Jesus's day (as will be seen in **Part II: The King**) and their chief end is to absolve themselves of the personal responsibility of discipleship. By dealing with God in an abstract manner, the abstract theologian avoids the confrontational nature of the Exodus, Jesus, and the gospel. Constantly bombarded with the reality of unjust suffering and limited educational resources, the black church saw "loving service to others as an emulation of God's love of humankind that is manifested primarily in the biblical picture of Jesus's earthly ministry to 'the least' of his sisters and brothers."[10] By experiencing unmerited suffering, the black church was reminded of Christ experientially and existentially. Simultaneously, the black church became the womb under which many social uplift initiatives were born. Jesus cares for the least of these, and helps those in need. The Political Christian ought to learn from the African American tradition by reminding the

---

[9] Gayraud S. Wilmore, *Pragmatic Spirituality: The Christian Faith through an Africentric Lens,* (New York: New York University Press, 2004), 4.

[10] Wilmore, *Pragmatic Spirituality*, 4-5.

church of its social imperative, and reminding the church of the ever-changing waters of public policy.

Since just policy is a moving target, and since improvement suggests the continuation of some unjust systems, one could see political policy as religious compromise. Here, the Political Christian must distinguish their contractual and covenantal commitments. The Political Christian must not compromise their religious duties, but they may strategically compromise on politics in the struggle to achieve moral ends. Reason and revelation are not enemies; they are brothers of the same Father. The Political Christian will have to use both in their duplex commitment, but they must make revelation the horse and reason the cart. Morality should shape one's political compromise. If reason is put before the horse (morality), the Political Christian can excuse any evil with logic.

When it is understood that pragmatic means are distinct from moral ends it becomes clear there is a space of personal responsibility that no government can fulfill. Martin Luther King Jr. is often characterized as a socialist that pushed for federal action to bring about change, but this portrait of King is reductionistic, misleading, and wrong. Jim Crow laws were institutionalized discrimination laws at the local, county, and state level. Despite the federally binding laws that should have outlawed Jim Crow laws, states continued to ignore the Civil Rights Amendments without accountability from the Executive Branch. King led grassroots movements using nonviolent direct action to call upon to government to enforce its own laws and eventually create laws more directly targeted toward discrimination. King did not sift personal responsibility to the government; he led a movement where everyone in the community took personal responsibility to bring about change. In fact, the African American tradition does not lack an ethic of self-responsibility with such figures as Frederick Douglas, Booker T. Washington, Malcolm X, and of course Martin Luther King Jr. just to name a few. All were promoters of self-reliance and the dignity of work. However, all knew that removing roadblocks for people was necessary for progress. Self-responsibility and collective political efforts are not competing realities. Collective efforts, when righteous can prefigure the beloved community. More importantly than King's boycott, ending discrimination laws, and eliminating racism was his ultimate vision rooted in God's eschatological beloved community.

Chapter 5

Regulating Pragmatism

And when they were in the field, Cain rose up against his brother Abel and killed him.
Genesis 4:8

We are bound together in a single garment of destiny. The language, the cultural patterns, the music, the material prosperity and even the food of America are an amalgam of black and white.
Martin Luther King Jr., *Where Do We Go From Here?*

Some may say that I am infantilizing the role of policy by labeling politics as merely pragmatic when it is clear that policy can result in humanitarian crises such as North Korea, Venezuela, Afghanistan, and other countries. But what I want to distinguish is pragmatic as a first principle and pragmatic as a helpful political tool. Politics is not foundational to morality. Morality can exist within an 'I-thou' framework apart from a political system. As a foundational moral ethic for social life, the golden rule is the surest foundation in God's created order. This law reflects the natural law God has woven into His creation. If followed, the golden rule suggests prohibitions and prescriptions that can be obeyed. No one wants to be raped, pillaged, and enslaved. Everyone wants love, acceptance, and a place to call home. It is quite clear from the golden rule alone that societies and governmental systems can be built. The golden rule is self-proving because of the goodness that it creates. Politics must presume the golden rule as a moral axiom and therefore eliminate any laws that do not reflect this axiom. Cornel West articulates a philosophy of prophetic pragmatism "whose focus is on coping with transient and provisional penultimate matters yet whose hope goes beyond them."[11] West's version of prophetic pragmatism is informed by the African American spiritual tradition who focused on providing spiritual hope and changing political structures. Biblical principles such as the golden rule must inform

---

[11] Cornel West, Edited by Louis Menand, "Prophetic Pragmatism," in *Pragmatism: A Reader,* (New York: Vintage Books, 1997), 413.

social reform. The golden rule becomes the relegating principle of pragmatism, which is to say pragmatism must be limited in its application.

Once the golden rule is established as a first principle, it is clear that neighbor exploitation is unacceptable. Instead, the golden rule suggests the well-being of the 'I-thou' are not in competition with one another but are actually bound up in one another. To exploit one's neighbor is to degrade both the 'I' and 'thou.' One of the biggest lies in society is that political resentment can lead to societal good. In no way, shape, or form is it morally acceptable to categorically condemn people on the basis of ethnicity, class, or tribal membership, for this eliminates the personalized 'I-thou' into a depersonalized 'us-them.' Nativist ideologies otherize groups as an act of tribal preservation. Nativism ultimately idolizes and absolutizes ethnicity and a sense of peoplehood over the priority of the gospel. Nativism will be dealt with more thoroughly in **Part II: The King**.

It is a fear of mine that one of the extremes created in response to nativism, is an antiracism polemic reacting against white supremacist structures. Solidarity is the new form of racial justice where people identify with the lowly and oppressed at a political level and distance themselves from the privileged. The biggest concern I have for this movement is a regression into an us-them framework. Since antiracism is a negative framework it has a fundamentalist tendency to overly racialize issues and does not have a vision for lasting racial peace. The reason why many people promote antiracism is because it deconstructs the notion of colorblindness. Colorblindness is an approach to racial issues that one should not acknowledge another person's skin color or culture. This myth promotes an idealized society that has never existed in the United States because the nation nor the laws have ever been colorblind. We have to recognize racialized issues without promoting racialized solutions that will fuel tribal instinct.

George Yancey says we need a new path that is neither antiracist nor colorblind in his book *Beyond Racial Division*. Foundationally, one issue that needs to be addressed is that the United States is racialized, which is to say we are heavily invested in race.[12] Even the most avid

---

[12] George Yancey, *Beyond Racial Division: A Unifying Alternative to Colorblindness and Antiracism,* (Downers Grove: Intervarsity Press, 2022), 18.

promoters of colorblindness may switch tunes if asked if they would permit their daughter to date a black man. Promoters of Afrocentrism and Black separatism would also express distaste over interracial marriage with white people. The reason why we still place value on race is because of the legacy of segregation and slavery. Our instincts toward race are tribal. This is why the Democratic Party can successfully campaign on the insecurities of the black community. This is why the Republican Party can successfully campaign on nativism. Society is racialized because we believe the interests of white people and black people are in competition. Instead, Yancey advocates for mutual accountability where, "we fashion solutions to racialized problems that address the needs of individuals across racial groups instead of promoting solutions that are accepted only by certain racial groups."[13] One possibility could be to pursue ministry and social programs that address economic issues meant to help all people groups. The SCLC understood that racial and economic discrimination were twin pillars of oppression. Toward the end of his life, King organized the Poor People's Campaign which sought the unify

---

[13] Yancey, *Beyond Racial Division*, 35.

white, black, Latino, indigenous, and Asian Americans on the issue of poverty. On a primary level, King's public issue was economics. On a secondary level, he was unifying people across racial lines.

Healing racially can only happen as an epiphenomenon since the instincts that divide us cannot be recycled into solutions to unite. When addressing the ethnic divide between Jews and Gentiles, the Apostle Paul commends Christ as the phenomenon that brings about unity. Unity is a byproduct of faith and transformation in Christ. He states Christ "has made us both one and has broken down in his flesh the dividing wall of hostility … that he might create in himself one new man in place of the two … and might reconcile us both to God in one body through the cross, thereby killing the hostility." (Eph. 2:14-17). First, Paul acknowledges the ethnic and religious division. There is a problem between Jews and Gentiles that needs to be addressed. Second, he does not eliminate distinction in the new body of Christ as the solution. In other words, the New Testament does not promote colorblindness as a healing ideology. There are still differences, but Christ is valued above all differences.

Third, Paul points to the phenomenon of Christ and His atonement which unifies without eliminating diversity.

To be clear, solidarity plays a role in creating a socially aware people, but it is a dead end without a proper moral path to interpersonal integration. Racial reconciliation can never be achieved through an 'us-them' framework because personality is depersonalized by tribalism. The natural law reveals that morality and reason are objective goods beyond individuals or groups. It is clear to me that this new form of identity politics does not have the political hold that some may fear, but it is my concern that the promoters of identity politics have a moral hold on people looking for a solution to the race problem. The new path of interpersonal living must relate to people within an "I-thou" framework that also considers their cultural background. After all, if one wants to see another they must see them for who they truly are, which includes their family, nation, and communities.

If one sees his brother as his competition instead of his ally the only resort he is left with is dominance. Rather than Cain repenting and recognizing his own sin and failings, he blamed his brother. Cain saw Abel as the enemy holding him back rather than as his brother made in God's image. As the King quote reminds us, "We are bound together in a single garment of destiny."[14] The future of all humanity depends on all humanity. As Desmond Tutu's book reminds us, there is *No Future Without Forgiveness.*

There is no such thing as segregated history, nor is there such a thing as a segregated future because we are all interconnected. Freedom and well-being are collective enterprises; selective freedom is tyranny. The Political Christian must have, as his scope, the common good rather than his special interest groups. However, if one group is prioritized as more vulnerable than another, this does not negate the value of the less vulnerable in God's eyes. Instead by lifting up a brother in need, both he and his neighbor are brought closer to God. But neighbor love goes beyond self-interest. Just mercy bridges the justice and love of God and unites divided people. If all humanity is made in God's image then loving humanity is an expression of loving God. If one cannot love his fellow human, this begs the question if the Political Christian loves God at all.

---

[14] Martin Luther King Jr, *Where Do We Go From Here: Chaos or Community?* (Boston: Beacon Press, 2010), 54.

Chapter 6

Pursuing the Dream

Now the church, I believe, ought to be a pilot plant in regard to the healing of man and himself, of man and man, and man and nature.
> Francis Schaeffer, *Pollution and the Death of Man*

But declarations against segregation, however sincere, are not enough. The church must take the lead in social reform. It must move out into the arena of life and do battle for the sanctity of religious commitments. And it must lead men along the path of true integration, something the law cannot do.
> Martin Luther King Jr., *Where Do We Go From Here?*

The gap that no law, government, or boycott could fill was brotherhood among men. In King's final book published in 1967, *Where Do We Go From Here?,* he makes the distinction between "enforceable" and "unenforceable" ethics. King states, "Genuine integration will come when men are obedient to the unenforceable. Dr. Harry Emerson Fosdick has made an impressive distinction between enforceable and unenforceable obligations. The former are regulated by the codes of society and the vigorous implementation of law-enforcement agencies… But unenforceable obligations are beyond the reach of the laws of society."[15] While the government can enforce laws that promote integration in schools, workforces, and government positions, the government cannot create brotherhood. Integration has very political connotations. To clarify his vision, he uses the term "interpersonal." As a theological personalist, King believed the most sacred essence in all of life was personhood because all personality was grounded in the Godhead. He writes, "Court orders and federal enforcement agencies are of inestimable value in achieving desegregation, but desegregation is only a partial, though necessary, step toward the final goal which we seek to realize, genuine intergroup and interpersonal living."[16]

---

[15] King, *Where Do We Go From Here?*, 105-6.

Here he reveals that all along the laws that eliminated the "I-it" and "us-them" living were only the means to bring out the end of ethics— "I-thou" living.

The Christian response to culture is involvement, not disengagement, because the gospel changes individuals and societies. So often, the void of the church creates an easy vacuum for extremists to enter. To those that say we must merely "preach the gospel," they ought to consider the words of James: "If a brother or sister is poorly clothed and lacking in daily food, and one of you says to them, 'Go in peace, be warmed and filled,' without giving them the things needed for the body, what good is that? So also faith by itself, if it does not have works, is dead" (Jm. 2:15-17). Christian ethics goes far beyond politics, personal sentiment, and mental assent because Christianity deals with direct loving relationships. The gospel of Christ demands action and community. Francis Schaeffer, in his book *Pollution and the Death of Man* (1970), gives the analogy that the church is like a pilot plant for the larger society. A pilot plant is a small test plant companies use before they expand to grand-scale production. If we accept this analogy, the church must live out biblical ethics

---

[16] Ibid., 106.

through local churches and micro institutions. Only after the local church lives out its commitment directly in their community should they consider larger-scale political change. In the pilot plant model, the church is the pacesetter and not the culture.

Despite King's imperative for the church to lead the way in integration, King's primary ministry toward the end of his life was political activism. I am not condemning King; King was the necessary leader during a time when the church lost its direction. He understood the societal outcome of Christianizing the culture but he forgot the means by which the early church moved mountains— the historic gospel of Jesus. Moreover, the *DoNothingism* of white America was unacceptable and white supremacy remained the biggest obstacle to racial reconciliation. What the church should have done during political segregation is integrating local churches. It is a tragedy that after the civil rights movement the church continued to be divided over race. Grassroots integration would have left the church free to live out the gospel in their communities regardless of whatever political climate existed. The reality is, by implementing political integration without addressing the spiritual division between white and black Americans, this created a false idea that unity is about outward appearance rather than inner transformation. Unity in the Christian sense, is not uniformity but familial union with Christ.

Christ's person and ministry embody both particular affirmations of culture and his universal representation of all humanity. Roberts states, "The genius of the Christian religion is that it is at once particular and universal, personal and social."[17] God became a man but He also became a Jewish man. At the wedding of Cana, Jesus involved Himself in a cultural dispute over hospitality. The hosts of the wedding did not have enough wine for the guests which would have resulted in social shame. Jesus saved the family from shame by providing more than enough wine for everyone, showing that disciples can embody some aspects of their cultural context (John 2:1-10). Jesus affirmed Jewish ethnicity, but He did not make ethnicity absolute or conditional in salvation. In fact, Jesus even broke some Jewish customs to show higher allegiance to God (see Lk. 11:38). Further

---

[17] J Deotis Roberts, *Liberation and Reconciliation: A Black Theology,* (Louisville: Westminster John Knox Press, 2005), 68.

proving Jesus's ethnic inclusion, Jesus set the foundation for Paul's apostleship for the gentiles when He said, "I have other sheep that are not of this fold. I must bring them also, and they will listen to my voice" (John 10:16). Jesus shifted the centripetal movement of the Old Covenant where the nations were drawn to Israel as their means to join God's covenant, to a centrifugal movement of the New Covenant where believers are to go to the nations as a prophetic minority. In other words, there is no geopolitical center in the New Covenant—only Christ.

In God's salvation history, He chose Jesus to represent all of humanity as the new Adam of a new humanity adopted by the Holy Spirit. The Apostle Paul declares, "Christ Jesus came into the world save sinners," and that there is "one mediator between God and men, the man, Christ Jesus" (1 Tim 1:15; 2:5). Christ, although a particular Jewish man, represented all of humanity at the cross. Since Christ died for the world, the mission of all Christians is to make disciples of all nations by teaching, baptizing, and going in the name and power of the Holy Trinity (Matt. 28:18-20). Jesus is making a giant, global family of brothers and sisters.

It is fair to say that King would agree with the assessment that integration did not go far enough based on his distinction between enforceable ethics and unenforceable ethics. Since there is a gap between the enforceable and unenforceable, Christians must not confuse the shallow waters of political integration but continue to the deep pools of Christian brotherhood. In the end, the moral arc bends to God's vision where people from all backgrounds and walks of life will worship Christ together in unity. John writes, "After this I looked, and there before me was a great multitude that no one could count, from every nation, tribe, people and language, standing before the throne and before the Lamb" (Rev. 7:9 NIV). There will never be an ideal society apart from the grace of God because of the sinfulness and finiteness of human nature. God will ultimately fill all the gaps between people and Himself. The way to Jericho will always be bloody, but it is never too late to start cleaning the way for Christ's return.

Part II
The King

The Good Samaritan in the Public Square
Interpreting Luke 10:25-37

> For the LORD your God is God of gods and Lord of lords, the great God, mighty and awesome, who shows no partiality and accepts no bribes. He defends the cause of the fatherless and the widow, and loves the foreigner residing among you, giving them food and clothing. And you are to love those who are foreigners, for you yourselves were foreigners in Egypt.
> Deuteronomy 10:17-19

Admittedly, I have not set a goal to prove every single point in this book. For example, while I know John Locke is by no means a perfect political theorist, I find his social contract theory compelling, and more importantly, so does Western culture. Lockean ideas are foundational and informative, but not perfect. Ultimately, I have set in motion principles that answer how we are to construct a political theology in a fallen world. The pragmatics of

Christian ethics will have to change with each generation but the theology will be the same. As such, the duplex principles should be viewed as wisdom to be tested out, not law to be trusted in. Using the analogy of a car, if the principles get you from point A to point B, then use them. If you find the principles get you halfway and need repair, take them back into the shop, find out what's wrong, and fix them. If the principles are not helpful at all, throw them out altogether. Nonetheless, this section of the book seeks to answer the question of biblical interpretation. How does Jesus command His disciples to live in different social spheres in life? Does Jesus merit a political theology, or was He an advocate of apolitical theology?

In the parable of the Good Samaritan, Jesus condemns socioreligious indifference toward the "poor" (the word will be defined as vulnerable) within a racially divided society, instead advocating for personal involvement in the life of the poor for the purpose of restoration and brotherhood. If one is to understand the parable, it is important to understand the Deuteronomic Code God gave to the Israelites with how they were commanded to treat the vulnerable. The parable is not just for personal application but it is a social commentary on

God's covenant people and racial division. Lastly, to understand the parable, we must see the development from neighborhood to brotherhood in God's salvation history. Part of what it means to be a good neighbor is to share the gospel because the lost and unreached people groups are the most vulnerable in society. Only through Christ can ultimate brotherhood be realized.

What follows is an exposition of the Good Samaritan passage with the following headings: Luke 10:25-29 Jesus dialogues with an abstract theologian. Vv. 30-35 Jesus dissents from spiritual indifference. Vv. 36-37 Jesus disciples toward compassionate restoration.

Chapter 7

Jesus & the Abstract Theologian

Luke 10:25-29 Jesus dialogues with an abstract theologian. Jesus upset the masses, especially the religious establishment, so they always wanted to trap Jesus to seek out His flaws rather than repent of their own. This dialogue with an expert in the law fits a pattern seen in the gospels. A religious expert, under the assumption that Jesus will somehow contradict the Law, will ask a theological question with the motive to find a flaw in Jesus (Matt. 22:23-28, 22:34-36, Mark 12:13-15, John 8:4-6). Usually, Jesus responds to the trap with a discussion of the Law revealing the sin in His opponent (Matt. 22:29-31, 37-39, Mark 12:15-16, John 8:7). Lastly, Jesus develops the Law to a further theological point, raising the standard of the Law, showing Jesus's moral perfection and divine insight (Matt. 22:32, 40, Mark 12:17,

John 8:7,11). The expert of the Law asked Jesus what to do to inherit eternal life (v. 25) and the first alarming concern is that Jesus brings up the Law (v. 26). Since no one can live out the Law perfectly, it is odd Jesus immediately commands the expert to obey the Law. What is the purpose of the Law in evangelism? The Law reveals the character of God (Ex. 34:6), the sinfulness of man (Rom. 7:7), and points to Jesus as the perfect embodiment of the Law (Matt. 5:17, Rom. 10:4). When Jesus affirms the Two Great Commandments—love God with all your heart, and love your neighbor as yourself (v. 27)— Jesus is trying to reveal personal and social sin for the purpose of evoking repentance.

Embarrassed that Jesus reaffirmed Jewish morality, and thus avoiding the trap, he asked "And who is my neighbor?" (v. 29). It is very likely this religious expert narrowed the definition of neighbor to exclude Samaritans because they were not pure-blooded Jews. Jesus, in the Sermon on the Mount, condemned religious leaders who amended the second greatest command, "You have heard that it was said, 'You shall love your neighbor and hate your enemy'" (Matt 5:43). In Jesus's time, religious people found many reasons to narrow the love-ethic for a myriad of excuses. Jesus expanded the ethic of love to the most extreme so as to remove any exception clauses, "But I say to you, Love your enemies and pray for those who persecute you, so that you may be sons of your Father who is in heaven" (Matt. 5:44-45). If disciples are to love even enemies then there is no exception to who they can love. In Jesus's parable, the precise purpose of making the hero of the story an "impure" Samaritan, and sidelining the socioreligious elite, is to centralize the marginalized; prioritize the belittled; to recognize the forgotten. Jesus centers the least of these: the hungry, the thirsty, the foreigner, the naked, the sick, and the imprisoned (Matt. 25:35-36). Jesus Himself was marginalized as one who was born in a manger, almost killed by Herod as a baby, sojourned to Egypt, was poor, and was eventually executed on a Roman cross by the religious elite. Jesus humanizes the least of these through the passion, showing that the most vulnerable still have dignity and worth. To those who feel like damaged goods, Jesus says, "You matter! You're important!" Jesus is revealing the unloving heart of the questioner who seeks to narrow the definition of love. By doing so, Jesus is revealing sin in the religious expert to show his need for mercy. This is true of every sinner. No matter how loving one may think of themselves, our sinful nature will always seek to narrow the command to love one's neighbor.

In addition to revealing the questioner's sin, Jesus is also redefining how one does theology. Jesus prioritizes the application of the Word over-intellectualized theology. Jesus condemns the religious elite for utilizing the Word of God for their own selfish purposes, and to make themselves the center of God's universe:

> For they preach, but do not practice. They tie up heavy burdens, hard to bear, and lay them on people's shoulders, but they themselves are not willing to move them with their finger. (Matt. 23:3-4)

> Woe to you, scribes and Pharisees, hypocrites! For you tithe mint and dill and cumin, and have neglected the weightier matters of the law: justice and mercy and faithfulness. (Matt. 23:23)

> You have a fine way of rejecting the commandment of God in order to establish your tradition! For Moses said, 'Honor your father and your mother'; and, 'Whoever reviles father or mother must surely die.' But you say, 'If a man tells his father or his mother, "Whatever you would have gained from me is Corban"' (that is, given to

> God)—then you no longer permit him to do anything for his father or mother, thus making void the word of God by your tradition that you have handed down. And many such things you do. (Mark 7:9-13)

Jesus's condemnation is not against Judaism anymore then His words are a condemnation for Christianity today. Jesus is condemning the immorality of God's professing covenant people who are supposed to be the stewards of God's revelation. Jesus affirms the morality of the Old Testament but condemns those who minimize the central matters to God's Law. To be sure, Jesus is not advocating an anti-intellectual theology either. Theology is more than the life of the mind; it is a lived experience where Jesus invades the believer's life. On the other hand, religious elites camouflage their agendas with the Word of God to appear religious but inside are full of dead men's bones (Matt. 23:27). These lost people may have God's Word on their lips, but they do not have the Word of God in their hearts. So, while loving one's neighbor may seem intellectually self-evident, according to Jesus, one has not yet understood the Law if they still hold the prejudices of their sinful nature that narrow the scope of God's love.

It may be uncomfortable to acknowledge where the church has had culpability in racial discrimination, *de facto* segregation, sexual abuse, abuse coverup, homophobia, sexism, and indifference to the poor, and many have denied these realities. Some fear that acknowledging these past wrongs is dangerous out of a larger concern of theological Liberalism. Wouldn't acknowledging past oppression usher in a leftist, woke agenda? The answer to this question is no. Moreover, if repenting of religious legalism and embracing the poor is perceived as leftist then so be it; discipleship comes with scorn. We ought not to concern ourselves with perceptions beyond our control. It is time for Christians to take the parable of the Good Samaritan seriously by seeking the best interest of the least of these, rather than preserve the status of the greatest of these.

Chapter 8

The Broken Road

Vv. 30-35 Jesus dissents from spiritual indifference. Jesus responds to the expert's question, which presumed a narrow definition of neighbor, with a story for the purpose of changing the question. The question is not, "who is my neighbor?" (intellectual). The question is, "am I a neighbor?" (practical). By the end of the story, it will be clear how Jesus has shifted the question. To change the question, Jesus begins with the exposition, "A man was going down from Jerusalem to Jericho" (v. 30). The man in question is unnamed to suggest universal application—he can be any man because stories like this happen every day. The vague "he" is traveling from a very specific city, Jerusalem, the sacred city of the Jews. Priests, experts of the law, the Temple, and the overall religious identity of the Jews were found in

Jerusalem. If Jesus told the story today He might choose a symbolic city like Rome, or a prominent city church, where God's people can be found in high numbers. The man traveling was headed to Jericho, which would have been understood to have been dangerous. Picture someone walking through a high crime area at night. Jesus's audience would have known that the man in question is in danger.

Next is the rising action, where conflict enters the story: "and he fell among robbers, who stripped him and beat him and departed, leaving him half dead" (v. 30). In the New Testament, Jesus shows recognition for the despised, rejected, and hated of society so it is no surprise He tells a story about a man who fell among robbers. Poor can be interchangeable with vulnerable. In the west, we think poverty is monetary. Poverty is not a monetary issue, it is a spiritual issue brought by the Fall. For this reason, Christians should adopt the language of "the vulnerable" of society. Jesus is forcing us to ask the question: Who are those in danger? The widow? Orphan? Unwanted pregnancy? Drug addict? Veteran? The least of these are the people Jesus has called the church to minister to. The man in this story is poor in the sense he is in danger with no one to help him. He is left for dead on a dangerous road where many of God's people could help him. He is naked and humiliated, much like Christ was on the cross. The fact is, without someone to help this man, he will die. Poverty is not about money—it is about life and death.

A point detrimentally missed in liberation theologies is a failure to recognize unreached people groups as the most vulnerable because of the terrible legacy of colonization. Unreached people groups (UPGSs) are those without access to the gospel and will therefore die in their sins without forgiveness. This means UPGs will die eternally separated from God. To those who say, "isn't that unfair?" would do well to remember that grace is not fair. Salvation is a gift of God. Jesus graciously took on the wrath of God for humanity—that is not fair. We must tread carefully when climbing the slopes of what is fair and what is not, for in doing so we are ultimately placing ourselves on the throne rather than God. The last point to consider: salvation and damnation are not matters of knowledge or ignorance. Salvation is a matter of trust or pride. It is important to state, Christians are not intellectually or spiritually superior to unbelievers because salvation is a gift, not a reward. Since "the person without the Spirit does not accept the things that come from the Spirit of God" the Spirit of God, in an act of supernatural grace, must renew the heart. Paul continues, "the person with the Spirit makes judgments about all things" meaning the person with the Spirit is able to follow Christ (1 Cor. 2:14-15 NIV). Therefore, someone is only a Christian because of the power of the Spirit who enabled them to believe.

According to the Apostle Paul, people are not damned because of pedigree, or lack of knowledge, but because humanity knows God and rejects Him: "For although they knew God, they did not honor him as God or give thanks to him, but they became futile in their thinking, and their foolish hearts were darkened" (Rom. 1:21). Depravity is not a deficiency in the brain, but a sickness of the heart. Lost people are described as spiritually dead and following after Satan (Eph. 2:1-3). Thankfully, God loves the lost. Jesus describing His own ministry declared, "For the Son of Man came to seek and to save the lost" (Lk. 19:10). Echoing the commission of Christ, the Apostle Paul proclaims: "'Everyone who calls on the name of the Lord will be saved.' How, then, can they call on the one they have not believed in? And how can they believe in the one of whom they have not heard?" (Rom. 10:13-14 NIV). The gospel brings qualitative change to the human heart. The man who fell among robbers would have died without help. Maybe this is not fair, but living in a fallen world is not fair. If one accepts Jesus's line of reasoning on poverty as a matter of life and death why would this change with the gospel? If the name of Christ saves then those who die without Christ are damned. I do not feel good about damnation. In fact, my heart breaks that there are 3 billion people who will go to hell, but this only means the church must increase its efforts, not weaken the gospel.

God has commissioned the church with the power of the gospel and the Holy Spirit to reach UPGs with the gospel. It is up to the saved of those regions to "indigenize" the gospel and make it their own, rather than adopt Euro-American practices. Roberts defines indigenizing the gospel as recognizing the particularities of a specific context: "Theology cannot be truly universal if it refuses to deal with the particularities of the human situation. It must not, however, rest with the particular—it must move from the particular to the universal. In moving to the universal, it must abandon the *concrete* particular, for there is where we meet the human situation."[18] Whiteness has wrongly taken the place of universality in many theologies, but Christianity teaches that God, the universal, became a particular Jewish man. Since all people are made in God's image, what is not sin is a picture of God's diversity throughout the world. God's creatures have freedom, in Christ, to express their faith within their culture, so as long as they are not in sin. Now that vulnerability has been rightly defined, ministry can be defined as tending to the needs of the body and soul. Christ is concerned with the whole man.

Jesus continues the ongoing drama of life and death: "Now by chance a priest was going down that road, and when he saw him he passed by on the other side. So likewise a Levite, when he came to the place and saw him, passed by on the other side" (vv. 31-32). Conflict in the story of the Good Samaritan is not about perpetrators of commission but complicit perpetrators of omission. Said more simply, Jesus's dissent is not about the robbers

---

[18] J. Deotis Roberts, "Contextual Theology: Liberation and Indigenization," *Christian Century,* January 28, 1976, pgs. 64-68.

because lost people are expected to act unjustly. Jesus's dissent is about those who call themselves "Jews" or "Christians" but do not reflect the character of God they believe in. For lack of a better term, the antagonists of the story are those who should have helped the man more than anyone. In the first place, a priest is someone called by God to represent God's people with sacrifices and offerings. A priest would have been reminded every day in the Temple of God's justice and His mercy. In the second place, because of the Levites's status as priests, they had a unique role in God's salvation history. The Levites had a special calling in Israel. They were the only tribe selected to play the role of mediator between God and man. Given this unique calling, the Levites should be more eager to serve others in need. Gratitude should have overflowed from their hearts onto the man forsaken, just as God did when He heard the cries of the Jews and rescued them from Pharaoh.

The Deuteronomic Code is one of the most beautiful parts in all of Scripture because the heart of God is revealed as one of compassion, the main attribute the Levites failed to demonstrate. In chapters 12-26 of Deuteronomy, God commands how His covenant people are to live collectively. For instance, in chapter 15, God commands Israelites to cancel debts after seven years (Deut. 15:1-18). Moreover, in the passage, God tells the Israelites to give generously to the poor since there will always be people in need (Deut. 15:11). God encourages generosity toward the vulnerable because the heart of God is one of compassion and rescue. Anyone who knows the financial burden of debt knows that debt leads people to make short-term financial decisions that often keep people in poverty. Debt also creates an unhealthy financial dependence, rather than financial interdependence. God's Law requires a cycle of cancelation to ensure no one is permanently ransacked by debts. This would also include indentured servants working off their debt to their masters. Clearly, God is regulating an often-abused system of servitude to limited times. Scripture speaks against live-long, racial, chattel slavery based on kidnapping. In fact, God rescued the Israelites from unjust, lifelong slavery.

Amazingly, God's rescue of the Israelites was meant to produce compassion towards their oppressors. Speaking against the sin of Cain and Abel, God implores, "You shall not abhor an Edomite, for he is your brother. You shall not abhor an Egyptian, because you were a sojourner in his land" (Deut. 23:7). Here, God is breaking down nativist hostility toward foreigners. The word sojourner is archaic, but the meaning is clear: someone who moves from one place to another. The NIV translates the word as "foreigner," but it could also be translated as "immigrant." Echevarria argues that God's people from the Old Testament to the New Testament have been called immigrants:

> Throughout redemptive history, God's people have been called immigrants, people sojourning to a place where Jesus will reign as king (Ezekiel 36-37; Isaiah 40-66; Revelation 20-22)… Along the way, Abraham's descendants became slaves in Egypt – in other words, poorly treated immigrants (Exodus 1-14)…. Peter, for example, calls his readers "*elect immigrants*" (1 Peter 1:1) and "*immigrants and sojourners*" (2:11), terms often used to refer to someone who is living in a foreign land, either by force or by their own volition.[19]

In the history of the Israelites, they were foreigners in the land of Egypt, and nomads in the desert before they reached the promised land. The Israelites were meant to learn from their experience of exclusion. Moreover, the

---

[19] Miguel Echevarria, "What does the Bible say about Immigrants?" *Biblical Recorder,* (Cary, NC), Feb. 19, 2018.

Israelites were even meant to love their despicable oppressors—the Egyptians. Sadly, the nativism of Jesus's day excluded Samaritans because they were not pure-blooded Jews, showing they did not learn from their experience of exclusion. When Jesus encountered the man with a narrow view of love, He reminded him that Samaritans are brothers.

Many Christians in the United States have been captivated by nativist and nationalist ideologies that fear immigrants as a threat to their culture and way of life. If American Christians adopt preservationist ideologies, this will lead many to ignore the refugees of the Middle East and the economic migrants of the South, worse yet, support policies that prevent vulnerable people from finding refuge in an affluent country with gospel access. As stated before, poverty is not about money. Poverty takes on many shapes and sizes because it is a cosmic battle of life and death. The reason why there are refugees, economic migrants, mass incarceration, and unwanted pregnancies is because of the war humans waged with God in the Garden of Eden. Sin has vastly corrupted this world, but the kingdom of God is at hand. Jesus has overcome the world and the church are His hands and feet to serve the needy. King Jesus says to North American Christians, "You have heard that it was said love your neighbor, but fear the immigrant, but I say unto you, the immigrant is your brother." Liberal theology ignores the gospel's role in ultimate brotherhood through Christ, but every person shares in the brotherhood of Adam. We all have the same Creator but not all of humanity knows the New Adam—Jesus. The Christian's job is to make the nations their "double-brother"—sibling by common Creator and by common Savior.

As it turns out, the Hebrew Bible beat Karl Marx to the finish line when it comes to concerns about the economically exploited. God forbids economic exploitation towards the needy, "You shall not oppress a hired worker who is poor and needy, whether he is one of your brothers or one of the sojourners who are in your land within your towns. You shall give him his wages on the same day, before the sun sets (for he is poor and counts on it)" (Deut. 24:14-15). In a sinful world, it is easy for the greatest of these to take advantage of desperate people simply because the desperate have no incentive to challenge their only source of income. Here, God commands the Israelites to treat all races fairly when it comes to payment. Many have been exploited out of money by religious people. This was true of Jesus's day, for Jesus condemns Pharisees for exploiting widows out of houses (Mk. 12:40), and Jesus overturned the tables of the money changers who were financially exploiting the poor in the name of God (Mk. 11:15-18). Since the Pharisees were able to financially ruin widows for the sake of wealth, it is clear that not all income inequality is natural or merited. Some poverty exists because of the unchecked power of the privileged.

Some may say that poverty is only a result of personal sin, and that the category of social sin is altogether unbiblical. However, if one takes the premise that there would not be poverty in a sinless world then this would have to mean that poverty is a result of the Fall. Adam's sin has a social element to it. Adam personally sinned but he did not sin into a vacuum. Adam's sin infected all of humanity. Sin is a cancerous disease that impacts and corrupts everything it touches. The Deuteronomic Code commands Israelites to live in a way that minimizes, and even prevents poverty. God is a God of love, and He has compassion for the downtrodden of society. As the Virgin Mary praises in the

Magnificat: "He has brought down the mighty from their thrones and exalted those of humble estate" (Lk. 1:52). God loves to help those in need, and this becomes vividly clear in salvation: "While we were still sinners, Christ died for us" (Rom. 5:8). Jesus put his life on the line for people who rejected Him, scorned Him, and were indifferent to his suffering. It is true we do not pray as we should, we do not read the Bible as we should, we do not give to the poor as we should, and yet God loves us right where we are at. The Levites had every reason to help the man in need: they had the Law of God (which reveals the character of God), they had a special calling to make them grateful to God, and they were rescued from the terrible clutches of Egyptian oppression. So where was the heart of compassion that God gave them? Why didn't they take the Deuteronomic code seriously? Why is it a temptation for God's covenant people to disengage the needy?

In answering the question of why the Levites did not stop to help the man who fell there can be several motives but all can be kept under the umbrella of indifference. Neither of the Levites hated the man who fell among robbers, they just did not care enough to involve themselves in an interpersonal way. Original sin has been deemed as selfishness by many, and in taking the role of bystander, the Levite reiterated the original sin of their spiritual forefather Adam. Martin Luther King Jr. reflects on the passage in the following way:

> In the days of Jesus [the road to Jericho] came to be known as the "Bloody Pass." And you know, it's possible that the priest and the Levite looked over that man on the ground and wondered if the robbers were still around. Or it's possible that they felt that the man on the ground was merely faking. And he was acting like he had been robbed and hurt, in order to seize them over there, lure them there for quick and easy seizure. And so the first question that the Levite asked was, "If I stop to help this man, what will happen to me?" But then the Good Samaritan came by. And he reversed the question: "If I do not stop to help this man, what will happen to him?"[20]

Part of helping the needy involves personal risk. For example, those involved in the foster care system know that involving yourself in the foster care system puts yourself and sometimes your family in danger. Still, many continue to fight through the obstacles of foster care because they know that children need loving parents as

---

[20] Martin Luther King Jr., "I See the Promised Land," *A Testament of Hope: The Essential Writings and Speeches*, (New York: HarperSanFransisco, 1991), 284-5.

much as they need food and water. The Levites may have been motivated to pass by because there was a possibility of risk. The Samaritan flips the paradigm by considering the needy in terms of life and death. If Christians refuse the call to engage with the life of a single pregnant mom, a disabled veteran, an out-of-work truck driver, or an inner-city drug dealer that person may die without knowing Jesus as their Lord and Savior.

Now, Jesus brings us to the turning point where the direction of the story is forever altered by an unlikely hero: "But a Samaritan, as he journeyed, came to where he was, and when he saw him, he had compassion" (v. 33). A Samaritan would not have had the right pedigree to be taken seriously in theological matters, but as it turns out the Samaritan had a much better theology than the Levites. What stands out about the Samaritan's theology? The Samaritan's theology was *1) relational, 2) affectionate, and 3) practical*; whereas the questioner and the Levite's theology was *1) uninvolved, 2) indifferent, and 3) abstract.*

Relational. While the Levites passed by the dying man, the Samaritan came to the man in need. This is because the Samaritan understood if he did nothing the man would die. In order to save him, the Samaritan had to involve himself in the life of his fellow image bearer. He did not defer responsibility to anyone else because God's Word is clear that everyone is called to help the needy— you do not need to be a missionary, pastor, or theologian to help the needy. Taking on the burdens of others is inconvenient, but discipleship requires dying to self. Just as Jesus poured Himself out for us, so we are to pour ourselves out for others.

Affectionate. Secondly, the Samaritan felt compassion for his fellow image bearer. Discipleship involves an inner spiritual life that does not reduce spirituality to the intellectual. Discipleship requires devotion from the head and heart. Christians would do well to model their devotion after King David, who cried out to God as a needy child. Political theology runs the risk of eliminating the devotional life altogether in the quest for social justice but the Samaritan started where we should all start—the character of God. The Levites ignored the message of God's salvation history, hardened their hearts, and passed by. The religious expert took a divine command and turned it into a religious abstraction. The Samaritan took the divine commands as a true story working itself into history. The Samaritan's compassion was a mere reflection of the goodness and kindness of God outworking in his life.

Practical. Lastly, the Samaritan's love was practical. It is not enough to have good intentions in matters of life and death. Again, this is not to say the Samaritan is a utilitarian. The Samaritan's baseline worldview is the second commandment: love your neighbor. Practicality comes into the picture when Christians use reason and faith together in complex situations. The Samaritan comes across a bloody, naked man, on the Bloody Pass, and if he does not act fast the man will die. Said more simply, the Samaritan has to use the brain God gave him. The Samaritan did not have to pray and ask God if the Samaritan needed medical assistance; it was self-evident. Using common sense is not a sin. In fact, once God regenerates a heart to embrace the gospel, the Christian is free to use common sense to apply to the Word of God in situations.

Jesus moves from the intention of the Samaritan to his practice in the falling action of the story: "He went to him and bound up his wounds, pouring on oil and wine. Then he set him on his own animal and brought him to an inn and took care of him" (v. 34). Helping the needy requires Christians to get messy. One has to imagine the hands of the Samaritan. His hands would have been bloody from wrapping bandages around bloody wounds; they would have been covered in oil and wine; his clothes dirty as he picked up an almost dead and placed him on his animal. There was nothing abstract about the Samaritan's love. His love was as real as Jesus. Jesus was the Word made flesh and dwelt among us. Jesus ate and dinned with sinners, a sign of acceptance and affection. Jesus healed the sick, cast out demons, and preached the kingdom through the material ears God gave humanity. Jesus died on a Roman cross, and was bodily resurrected. Jesus was not an abstract theologian—He was a servant to His own creation. Jesus, the Creator of heaven and earth, came to serve us and wash our feet. With such a great example, there is no lack of motive for the Christian to serve the vulnerable.

Lastly, the parable ends with the denouement, revealing the Samaritan's total commitment to helping those in need: "And the next day he took out two denarii and gave them to the innkeeper, saying, 'Take care of him, and whatever more you spend, I will repay you when I come back'" (v. 35). The parable of the Good Samaritan is not about the robbers, Levites, or the vulnerable; it is about the Samaritan's self-giving love. The Samaritan had good motives and good practices because Christians should be both rightly motivated and properly practical. It is not enough to feel compassion and do nothing for the needy. Jesus did not look at humanity indifferently and say, "Sorry." He took on flesh and involved Himself in the lives of sinners. Christian love is interpersonal. The Samaritan's love can be classified as *1) materialistic, 2) rational, and 3) total.*

Materialistic. Christianity has a healthy materialism because of the doctrine of creation. Many religious systems are antinature religions that require intense asceticism, esoteric mystical experiences, and a negative view of the body, placing value in the soul. Other religious systems can be classified as nature religions that place all value in the material world and often worship harvest gods. Since Christianity teaches that God created the material world, and declared the world to be good, and since God took on flesh, Christianity has a high view of the body. The Samaritan tends to the body God made because God is concerned with the whole man. Man does not live on bread alone, but he still lives by bread. When the Samaritan takes the dying man to the innkeeper, he does this so his body can rest and recover. Christians are not called to merely preach the gospel. They are called to embody the kindness of the Samaritan who cared for the whole man.

Rational. The love of the Samaritan is not divorced from his mind. The Samaritan, for whatever reason, was not able to tend to the dying man the whole time so he organized a helper. Here, it is clear that not all Christian ethics are direct action. A Christian will need help from others in order to help others. Reason will come to aid the Christian who have to use indirect means to bring about moral ends. The Samaritan, teamed with the innkeeper, was able to finish the task God called him to, by completely tending to the dying man. He vows to pay for any expenses, revealing that while poverty is not a monetary issue, there will still be expenses in the battle of life or death. Moreover, Christians should not minister alone. God calls each believer to be joined with a covenant community of believers for the purpose of making disciples together, and tending to the needs of the vulnerable.

Total. Love always goes the distance and in the parable, the Samaritan's love went all the way. In my high school carpentry class, there was a phrase my shop teachers would always tell us whether we were cleaning, sanding, or nailing something: "Don't half-a** any job." No matter the job we were assigned, we had to do the job well, and see it to the end. Mild vulgarity aside, everything we do should be done for the glory of God so we should see a commitment to the end. The Samaritan voluntarily committed himself to the dying man and he made sure he would be fully restored to health. The Samaritan vows to pay any expenses needed, showing consideration for the innkeeper as well as the dying man. Christians should work to completion, not for convenience.

The parable of the Good Samaritan finds itself in between the Deuteronomic code, and the New Testament ministry of spiritual brotherhood. In order to minister to the whole man, the gospel must be preached to break down the spiritual divisions that exist between Adam's children. The Apostle Paul reminds the newly grafted-in Gentiles of their status prior to God, "remember that you were at that time separated from Christ, alienated from the commonwealth of Israel and strangers to the covenants of promise, having no hope and without God in the world" (Eph. 2:12). Paul presumes that hope is only bound up with Christ, and the newly converted Gentiles were hopeless like the man who fell among robbers. Thankfully, God loves the lost, and Christ came in to disrupt our alienated lives, "But now in Christ Jesus you who once were far off have been brought near by the blood of Christ" (Eph. 2:13). In the first place, Jesus's death was a substitute for sinful humanity so they could draw near to God in relationship. Secondly, the atonement addresses the second command to love one's neighbor. The Apostle Paul continues describing Christ's atonement: "and might reconcile us both to God in one body through the cross, thereby killing the hostility" (Eph. 2:16). Sinful divisions are often good things made into God things. There are ethnic differences, but they are no reason for spiritual pride. Gifts from God are often used to create tribal relationships with neighbors.

Whatever, the reason for hostility, there is a better reason for unity—Christ. Believers do not share the same culture, the same ethnicity, or the same practices, but they share the same Christ. Unity is not uniformity. Believers are one but many (1 Cor. 12:12). Paul concludes, "So then you are no longer strangers and aliens, but you are fellow citizens with the saints and members of the household of God" (Eph. 2:19). Jesus came to create a family, not a club, and Jews and Gentiles alike all find themselves under the Lordship of Christ. The Apostle John writes, "But to all who did receive [Jesus], who believed in his name, he gave the right to become children of God, who were born, not of blood nor of the will of the flesh nor of the will of man, but of God" (John 1:12-13). Jesus's spiritual family is an affront to the tribalism of this world because Jesus's love knows no geographical, ethnic, political or linguistic limitations. Without the gospel, there will be a gaping hole in the quest to love one's neighbor for human frameworks will always be finite and exclusive. Christian brotherhood is the ultimate inverse of the question, "who is my neighbor?" because Jesus died for everyone, therefore no one is outside of God's love. Since every human is made in God's image, every creature is made for God. All of Adam's children are the same family, but we have estranged ourselves from God and each other because of sin. Jesus has called us back to the household of God.

Chapter 9

The New Jerusalem

Vv. 36-37 Jesus disciples toward compassionate restoration. Jesus speaks with a clarity that suspends all arguments. While the religious expert was trying to trap Jesus, Jesus tied the expert up into a story he could not escape. Now that Jesus has revealed the underlying sinfulness of the question "who is my neighbor?" He turns from the Samaritan to the expert and asks, "Which of these three, do you think, proved to be a neighbor to the man who fell among the robbers?" (v. 36). Notice how Jesus tries to involve the expert in the story, rather than let him redirect the story back to religious banter. The gospel always requires personal choice, not speculative conjecture. The expert cannot escape the question even if he refused to answer: "Am I a neighbor, or am I a bystander?" Neighbor is shifted from the status of another to the inner disposition of the heart. If the

Samaritan adopted the religious logic of the Levites, he would have never stopped to help the person in need. Religious indifference can be spotted when God's people distance themselves from God's Word as a spectacle to be discussed, rather than a script to be lived by.

Jesus's question was rhetorical, the Good Samaritan was a neighbor who took God's Word seriously. The expert, now made a novice by the Son of Man, admits "The one who showed him mercy" was a neighbor (v. 37). Apparently embarrassed by the Samaritan's "lower pedigree," the expert does not even mention the Samaritan by the title Jesus gave to him. Yet, the expert concedes that the Samaritan was the only one who showed mercy. Mercy, in this instance, does not refer to someone who is forgiven of just punishment. The Samaritan's estate was undeserved suffering in line with the book of Job. Mercy, in this instance, is compassion for those who suffer (v. 33). In Bryan Stevenson's book *Just Mercy: A Story of Justice and Redemption*, he observes there are a variety of applications for mercy. In response to unjust treatment, just mercy seeks to restore the broken person and society to wholeness. Such is a fitting description of the Samaritan.

In the instance of Walter McMillian, Walter was falsely accused, hastily arrested under flimsy evidence, and pushed quickly toward the death penalty. In an act of equal compassion and involvement as the Samaritan, legal attorney Bryan Stevenson involved himself in the life of Walter to provide legal aid. Miraculously, Walter was exonerated of all charges after a long legal journey. Stevenson explains that no one is without the need for mercy in an unjust world:

> The power of just mercy is that it belongs to the undeserving. It's when mercy is least expected that it's most potent—strong enough to break the cycle of victimization and victimhood, retribution and suffering. It has the power to heal the psychic harm and injuries that lead to aggression and violence, abuse of power, mass incarceration.[21]

In the case of Walter, he was undeserving of suffering, and the very thing his soul needed was mercy for his liberation. In the case of the institution that ruined Walter's life, they needed to give mercy to make themselves whole. In the instance of a society of bystanders, mercy is needed because indifference and

---

[21] Bryan Stevenson, *Just Mercy: A Story of Justice and Redemption*, (New York: Spiegel and Grau, 2014), 294.

cruelty are poisonous to the soul. One group is marked by the sins of commission; the other group is marked by sins of omission. Therefore, no one is left without needing mercy. Mercy is healing on the road of brokenness, on the Bloody Way to Jericho. Christianity exchanges the currency of deserve for love, and helps the broken without price. Love goes beyond the atmosphere of brokenness into the celestial heights of dignity and wholeness. No one is left without scars on the road to Jericho, but hopefully, there will be someone to bring us bandages. Whether or not one deserves the bruises, we are all in need of healing.

Without forgiveness, humanity is subject to repeat the same cycles of brokenness as our forefathers. In the wake of the Rwandan conflict, Father Ubald decided to forgive his enemies and preach the forgiveness, freedom, and healing power of Christ. In the 100 days of slaughter, Hutu extremists murdered about 800,000 people, including Hutus who allied with the Tutsis. Moreover, many of the Tutsi women were assaulted and raped. Ubald lost over 80 members of his family and 45,000 parishioners to the Rwandan genocide. As with all genocides, the Rwandan conflict preached brother against brother, and tribalism to rally people against fellow human beings. In cycles of vengeance and fear, fear of others reciprocates and repeats. The extremists' act of genocide was actually an act of self/tribal preservation. Since the Hutus were afraid of the Tutsis, the genocide was justified. As a result of the Rwandan conflict, the Tutsis were afraid of Hutus. If given the opportunity, Tutsis could also justify vengeance because they would be preserving their families by destroying an adversary. Not only does vengeance and murder create endless cycles of death, but the trauma of both the victim and the oppressor is carried into other relationships and families.

Father Ubald decided to enter into the brokenness of both his Hutu and Tutsi brothers bringing the message of the cross of Christ. First, Father Ubald resolved not to imitate the wounds which were inflicted on him. Often victims act out their traumas on themselves and others. Responding to brokenness with brokenness only creates more brokenness. There comes a decision where one has to draw a line in the sand, and decide, "I will not punish myself. I will not retaliate." If the decision to create a boundary between yourself and your brokenness is never made, one will be enslaved to the cycle of brokenness.

Next, Father Ubald had to process his emotions and traumas before God and others. Children of God are commanded to practice vulnerability, not idealistic sainthood. Children of God are honest with themselves so they can receive the truth of Christ. The Psalmists are great examples of emotional vulnerability over theological flexing. David inquires of God: "How long, O Lord? Will you forget me forever? How long will you hide your face from me?" (Ps. 13:1). Surely, David knew that God is omnipresent? Surely, David knew that God is by his side even in the midst of troubles? Surely, David knows that faith is the engine, and emotions are the subject themselves to truth? Why did David confess his doubt about God's presence in his life? If David was taking a theological test, he would have failed because God is present in both the highs and lows in life. Yet, faith is seen when sinners bring their struggles before God. Yes, David is doubting God's presence, but he brings his concerns to his heavenly Father. The Apostle Peter exhorts, "Give all your worries and cares to God, for he cares for you" (1 Pet. 5:7 [New Living Translation]). Faith and doubt are not antonyms in the Christian life. The antonyms a Christian must be aware of are faith and prayerlessness.

Prayerlessness says to God that you are in control, and you have a handle on your emotions and traumas, neither of which are true. In the New Testament, a father with a demon-possessed son asks Jesus to cast the demon out, for the son was prone to self-harming from childhood (Mk. 9:20-22). Jesus said that all things, including healing, are possible if the father believes (9:23). The father infamously cries out in desperation: "I believe; help my unbelief!" (9:24). In response to the father's faith, Jesus heals the demon-possessed son. Taking doubts to God and asking for help is an act of faith. We need help. We need God to take our anxieties and pain, for if we do not give our worries to God they will consume us. Asking for freedom from personal trauma is the first, second, and last step on the road toward healing. Healing is a process, and every day has enough worries. A survivor of trauma must not see their journey as an event, but a long journey of letting God's love care, nourish, and comfort them.

    Lastly, Father Ubald decided to voluntarily forgiven his oppressors, realizing that Jesus forgave his sins. Survivors and culprits need forgiveness. No one is perfect. No one has all the answers. We are limited, we make mistakes, and we betray our own principles.

Forgiveness is the very essence of freedom and salvation. Jesus says, "For if you forgive others their trespasses, your heavenly Father will also forgive you, but if you do not forgive others their trespasses, neither will your Father forgive your trespasses" (Matt. 6:14-15). The greatest need for every single person is to find the forgiveness of Jesus and be reconciled with their heavenly Father. Once a child of God opens their heart to the forgiveness of God, they find the strength to forgive. If someone retains their desire for revenge, they are estranging themselves from their Father in heaven who loves them and wants a relationship with them. Revenge toward self and others is a resolve to stay on the path of brokenness. Salvation is reconciliation with God.

How then can a survivor forgive their oppressor? Forgiveness is only possible when it is a liberating choice, not an act of compliance. If survivor forgives the culprit as an act of idealistic sainthood, they are not forgiving to have fellowship with God, they are forgiving because they have to. This is like a parent grabbing their child by the ear and making them say, "I'm sorry." The sorry is generated by fear, not freedom. If forgiveness is forced on a survivor, the cycle of brokenness continues without first dealing with the underlying trauma. For every moment the survivor revisits their anger toward their oppressor, they feel ashamed that their forgiveness was disingenuous. The shame creates distance from their heavenly Father, for the child of God has not first learned to be vulnerable with their Creator and Redeemer. A sinner must confess their need for God to take their pain and anxieties. Forgiveness has to be something the survivor does for their relationship with God. Father Ubald summarizes the gospel by saying, *forgiveness makes you free*:

> Free to be healed. Free to find peace. Free from the chains of hate and free. God is the author of all miracles; he is the one who heals. But we must open our hearts and prepare ourselves to receive that healing…You must open the door to your heart so that Jesus can come inside and bring peace and healing.[22]

Forgiveness and mercy are necessary on the road to Jericho because forgiving the robbers and abusers prevents more robbers and abusers from continuing the cycle. When Christ comes into the hearts of survivors, they are deciding to live out the reconciling mission of

---

[22] Ubald Rugirangoga, *Forgiveness Makes You Free: A Dramatic Story of Healing and Reconciliation from the Heart of Rwanda,* (Notre Dame: Ava Marie Press, 2019), xxvii.

Christ. Christ proclaims, "Behold, I am making all things new" (Rev. 21:5). It is Christ's love and power that is changing the hearts and relationships of many. It is Jesus who is setting the captives free; free from addiction, revenge, and hatred.

Jesus commissions the expert, and to any who have ears to hear, to be like the Samaritan: "You go, and do likewise" (v. 37). Jesus is a practitioner of mercy and forgiveness in a society of passive indifference. It is a difficult and overwhelming charge to commit our lives to the despised, rejected, and hated. Loving the vulnerable of society will mean a change in lifestyle, a new way of looking at the world, or sacrificing something we do not want to surrender. Forgiving our enemies for the sake of our relationship with our heavenly Father is sometimes a long, painful journey. But Jesus tells us, "The time is fulfilled, and the kingdom of God is at hand; repent and believe in the gospel" (Mk 1:15). The time of complacency is over because Jesus has risen from the dead. He has radically altered the course of human history through love and self-giving transformation. He has radically transformed countless people's lives; it is never too late for Him to transform yours. Repentance requires dying to self, but it is not worthy to be compared to the newness of life. I pray that Jesus sets you free from whatever is holding you back from following Him faithfully on the road to Jericho.

Bibliography

Boothe, Charles Octavius. *Plain Theology for Plain People.* Bellingham: Lexham Press, 2017. Introduction by Walter R. Strickland II.

Chesterton, G.K., "Introduction to the Book of Job." In *The Book of Job.* London: Cecil Palmer and Hayward, 1916.

—. "*Orthodoxy.*" In *The Three Apologies of G.K. Chesterton: Heretics, Orthodoxy & The Everlasting Man.* Bristol: Mockingbird Press, 2018.

Miguel Echevarria. "What does the Bible say about Immigrants?" *Biblical Recorder,* (Cary, NC). Feb. 19, 2018.

Hansberry, Lorraine. *A Raisin in the Sun.* New York: Vintage Books, 1994.

King Jr., Martin Luther. *A Testament of Hope: The Essential Writings and Speeches of Martin Luther King Jr.* New York: HarperSanFransisco, 1991. Edited by James Melvin Washington.

—. "I Have a Dream." *National Archives.* Aug. 28, 1963. https://www.archives.gov/files/social-media/transcripts/transcript-march-pt3-of-3-2602934.pdf

—. *Where Do We Go From Here: Chaos or Community?* Boston: Beacon Press, 2010.

Kuyper, Abraham, George Kamps, Translator. "Sphere Sovereignty." Inaugural Address at *Free University,* October 20, 1880.

Lewis, C.S. "The Abolition of Man." In *The C.S. Lewis Signature Classics: An Anthology of 8 C.S. Lewis Titles.* New York: HarperCollins, 2017.

Locke, John. *Second Treatise of Government.* Indianapolis: Hackett Publishing, 1980.

Michaels, Marguerite. "Billy Graham: America is Not God's Only Kingdom." In *Parade Magazine,* February 1, 1981.

Prager, Dennis. *Deuteronomy: God, Blessings, and Curses.* Washington D.C.: Regent Faith, 2022. Edited by Joseph Telushkin.

Roberts, J. Deotis. *Liberation and Reconciliation: A Black Theology.* Louisville: Westminster John Knox Press, 2005.

—. "Contextual Theology: Liberation and Indigenization." *Christian Century,* January 28, 1976, pgs. 64-68.

Rugirangoga, Ubald. *Forgiveness Makes You Free: A Dramatic Story of Healing and Reconciliation From the Heart of Rwanda.* Notre Dame: Ava Marie Press, 2019.

Schaeffer, Francis. *Pollution and the Death of Man.* Wheaton: Tyndale House, 2011.

Smith, James K. A. *Awaiting the King: Reforming Public Theology.* Grand Rapids: Baker Academic, 2017.

Stevenson, Bryan. *Just Mercy: A Story of Justice and Redemption.* New York: Spiegel and Grau, 2014.

West, Cornel, Edited by Louis Menand. "Prophetic Pragmatism," in *Pragmatism: A Reader.* New York: Vintage Books, 1997.

Wilmore, Gayraud S. *Pragmatic Spirituality: The Christian Faith through an Africentric Lens.* New York: New York University Press, 2004.

Yancey, George. *Beyond Racial Division: A Unifying Alternative to Colorblindness and Antiracism.* Downers Grove: Intervarsity Press, 2022.

About the Author

George Harold Trudeau is a high school English teacher. He graduated with a Bachelor of Arts in English from the College at Southeastern in Wake Forest, NC. He enjoys teaching Shakespeare, American Novels, and Poetry to his students. In their spare time, he and his wife Estefany enjoy traveling to cities and attending Sunday services at their church. You can find George reading C.S. Lewis books in coffee shops, or taking in the beauty of old churches with stained glass windows.

www.ingramcontent.com/pod-product-compliance
Lightning Source LLC
LaVergne TN
LVHW051559080426
835510LV00020B/3046